On Programming:
A how-to Guide

An introductory guide to writing computer programs well, regardless of programming language, and knowing they're right

Karl Schank

On Programming: A How-to Guide. By Karl Schank.

Copyright © 2024, Karl Schank. All rights reserved.

kspubs.com

Quotations and illustrations cited from Wikipedia are licensed via Creative Commons CC-BY licenses sourced via MS Word, unless otherwise noted.

Scripture quotations from Berean Standard Bible (BSB), public domain (see https://berean.bible/licensing.htm), unless otherwise noted.

Cover illustration of a magnetic memory core by author. Cover design by James A. Fowler.

Body text in Georgia font.

ISBN:

Preface

Dedication

To my family,

my church family,

and

my God

On Programming

Contents

Preface	vii
Introduction	1
Program Structure	3
Overall Structure of a Typical Program	7
Table of Contents (TOC) Outline of a Typical Program	9
Fundamental Programming Algorithm	11
Fundamental Structure Theorem	19
Three fundamental structures and how to use them	21
Three basic structures	21
Sequence	23
If-Then-Else (Conditional Execution)	33
Do-While (Iteration)	41
Valid Variants and Extended Control Structures	51
Why variants? 51	
Repeat-Until	53
Select Case	59
For-Loop (Counted loop)	67
For-Each (Object selection loop)	73
Recursion	75
One more construct	77
Subroutine	77
Unsafe Structures	79
"Danger, Will Robinson!" 79	
Avoid these pseudo-"structures"! 81	
Conclusion	87
What's next? 87	
Appendix 1 – Conversion of `Repeat-Until` to and from `Do-While`	89
Conversion of `Repeat-Until` to Sequence plus `Do-While`	89

    Conversion of `Do-While` into `If-Then` plus `Repeat-Until`   91

Appendix 2 – Variables, data types, and data structures   93
    Data types   93
    Data Shape   94
    Data structures   95
    Files and databases   98

Appendix 3 – More extended examples   99
    KWIC Index   99
    Table-driven Finite State Machine (FSM)   107
    Event-driven interactive Tic-Tac-Toe   113

Appendix 4 – Loop Invariants   119

Appendix 5 – A word on program maintenance and debugging   123

Appendix 6 – What is a computer?   129
    Von Neumann computer architecture   129
    Computers and Information Systems hierarchy   133
    Computer Layers and Levels of Abstraction   135

Appendix 7 – A brief introduction to systems analysis   137
    The Formal Systems Approach   138

Bibliographical Index   139

Index to Definitions   147

Acknowledgments   149

Author   151

Preface

I'm a programmer at heart. My first career was as a computer practitioner. My second was teaching college courses in computer science, information systems, IS management, and IT project management.

The first course in programming was too often poorly taught, introducing bad practices that had to be un-taught before good practices could be freshly taught. So I taught it "right" in the first place. A survey of the second programming course showed that my first-course students performed significantly better in the second course than did other students. That lent additional credibility to the methods herein.

This book now shares it with a wider audience of beginning programmers so that they can avoid bad practices and do it "right" in the first place. Additional tips from my (first) career spent in computing are also provided throughout this book.

A highlight of this book is extended examples constructed and shown step-by-step throughout this book.

– Karl Schank
San Antonio, TX
27.Apr.2024

On Programming

Introduction

This is a practical guide to **how to *do* programming.** Not the syntax of a particular programming language[1], but *how to write programs*[2]. In fact, how to write or code quality programs, and know that they're right. Part of the beauty of this approach is that this is timeless and language-independent. It is not made obsolete with every choice of a new language or every change or update to a language compiler.

What's more – the good news – is that it's simple! Like basketball, baseball, and most sports, it's largely a question of getting back to the fundamentals. (And then, of course, practice.)

> *"It is practically impossible to teach good programming to students that have had a prior exposure to BASIC: as potential programmers they are mentally mutilated beyond hope of regeneration."*
>
> – Edsger W. Dijkstra, Computer scientist, 1975

Professor Dijkstra's issues were with a now-ancient dialect of the *Basic* programming language, c.1975. His detailed concerns no longer apply to today's object-oriented *Visual Basic* and modern variants. Nevertheless, his point about learning to program is well taken and still valid. My experience is similar, although not limited to Basic nor to any particular programming language.

I have had many years experience teaching programming at the university undergraduate level and in managing and supervising a production programming organization. In all this, I have found that it is all too common to teach programming poorly. Programming instruction usually concentrates on the *syntax*[3] of a specific language (C, Java, Python, Fortran, Basic, etc.) rather than on the **process of *how* to write programs.** These language-oriented approaches are like teaching creative writing by giving someone a dictionary!

This is especially ironic. Many students take to the process, the logic, and the discipline like a duck to water. Yet many others find that the really tough nut to crack is not

---

[1] There are plenty of other useful books about that – glorified dictionaries of programming languages' syntax and how to use it. Along with this present book, you may also need such a manual for the syntax and details of your particular programming language.

[2] Computer programming is also known as program <u>coding</u>. It is the same as program <u>construction</u>. The three terms are synonymous.

[3] Syntax is the grammar and keywords of a specific programming language.

syntax. Rather, the difficulty is the **process** of developing the logic and structure of a program to solve a given problem. Unfortunately, that key part is what's so often missing.

Additionally, introductory programming courses often – quite inadvertently – teach poor to horrible programming technique. This must then be un-taught and then re-taught correctly at the next level. Worse, (as Dijkstra notes) it may do a lifetime of uncorrected harm. This book attempts to teach it right in the first place.

> *"When you first learn something, learn it the right way. When you first do it, you're actively thinking about it and you still have an easy choice between doing it in a good way and doing it in a bad way."*
>
> *-- Steve McConnell, Code Complete, 2004*

Writing programs can be just plain fun – but also frustrating[4]. Part of the frustration is exactly this. If poorly constructed in the first place, the coding, the debugging, and eventual maintenance (see "Appendix 5 – A word on program maintenance and debugging", p.123) will be difficult and not fun at all.

The purpose of this book is to explain how to write computer programs the right way, in any programming language, and know that they're right.

> *"Begin at the beginning, the king said very gravely, and go on until you come to the end. Then stop."*
>
> *– Lewis Carroll, Through the Looking Glass*

Let us begin, then, with the basic inherent structure of a program or a software system.

---

[4] See "The Joys of the Craft", especially, and also "The Woes of the Craft" in Fred Brooks' book *The Mythical Man-Month: Essays on Software Engineering*. You'll enjoy reading these sections.

[5] A *program* (or program *code*) is the set of detailed instructions that tell the computer hardware what to do and how to do it. Or as Dave Thomas and Andrew Hunt put it in *The Pragmatic Programmer*, "Programs are something that transform inputs into outputs"; that's their very purpose. *Software* is a collective noun meaning programs. Programs are software. Software is composed of programs, usually a system of related and intercommunicating programs.

Program Structure

"Good programmers have always done structured programming."
— Karen Hogan, late 1970s

"Success is all about consistency around the fundamentals."
— Robin Sharma

"You can practice shooting eight hours a day, but if your technique is wrong, then all you become is very good at shooting the wrong way. Get the fundamentals down and the level of everything you do will rise."
— Michael Jordan

"It is time to return to those core values, time to get back to basics...."
— John Major

A well-designed _program_[5] or _software_ system – like a book, a term paper, a building, or a machine – has a structure. It is developed via a plan, often hierarchically[6], in a top-down, step-by-step manner. It is not thrown together randomly or bottom-up, "by the seat of the pants", with little direction or prior thought. It is not started with overly small design components ("bricks", say) in hope we'll reach some vague and unstated goal (a building or structure).

English prose is not composed letter-by-letter, for example. Buildings are not designed brick-by-brick (although they may be constructed that way after having the design planned out in advance). Rather, English prose is composed hierarchically, following a guiding idea to develop the chapters, paragraphs, sentences, and words in their proper place, order, and function. Each piece has a function and use, and each contributes to the whole in its proper place. The lowest individual component is the word, not the individual letter.

Similarly, architects design buildings hierarchically by structural systems according to plan, not by individual bricks and bolts. As the great architects have taught us, "form

---

[5] A _program_ (or program _code_) is the set of detailed instructions that tell the computer hardware what to do and how to do it. Or as Dave Thomas and Andrew Hunt put it in _The Pragmatic Programmer_, "Programs are something that transform inputs into outputs"; that's their very purpose. _Software_ is a collective noun meaning programs. Programs are software. Software is composed of programs, usually a system of related and intercommunicating programs.

[6] A hierarchical structure is a top-down, superior to multiple subordinates structure like an organization chart. It usually implies that the subordinates are encompassed within the superior like subordinate organizational branches within a division of a company.

follows function" in design: The resulting external form is determined by the function or purpose that it is to accomplish. (The alternative might be to design a generic building without considering how it is to be used. That wouldn't be a very good fit.)

In the same way, we don't construct programs and software systems statement-by-statement with no prior plan for the function of each statement and how or why it contributes to the whole. Instead, programs are best designed hierarchically, in a top-down, stepwise manner according to function. Each indivisible structure is in its proper place, order, and purpose. Each structure has a function, use, and reason, and contributes to the whole in its proper place.

The basic indivisible building block of a program is the *structure* – not the individual programming language statement – just as the word, not the letter, is the basic building block for an English paragraph. And, as in architecture, "form follows function".

> *"Spaghetti code," non-structured programs, and bottom-up programming*
>
> We might mention that there is a (poor) alternative of sorts. We could build programs bottom-up, by the "seat-of-the-pants", writing code without thinking first, with no goal in mind; coding first and asking questions later. Often, this is done by first coding what we best know and understand (or like!) and later trying to fit or expand it into the whole. This alternative usually results in nearly unmaintainable, unreadable, unfixable "spaghetti code". It won't work right the first time – or probably the fiftieth time! Unfortunately, the nightmarish tangle of *spaghetti code* (whose flowchart looks like a bowl of spaghetti) is all too common in real-life programs. And such code is terrible indeed to try to maintain! Why would anyone *do* that?
>
> Programmers like to code. Sometimes they like to code more than they like to plan. Often, more than they like to document what they've done. So sometimes, they just jump right in and start coding, skipping the planning. But in the long run, writing spaghetti code takes far *more* trouble and effort. Proper construction of programs is not only effective, but is actually fairly easy. It may seem slower and more tedious at first, though that improves with practice. Yet it's infinitely better than endless debugging of problematic code that could have been designed and programmed correctly in the first place, if decent techniques were used.

"Nobody is really smart enough to program computers. ... The way you focus your intelligence is more important than how much intelligence you have."

-- Steve McConnell, *Code Complete*, 2004

This business of *structure*, of course, inherently implies discipline. In our modern culture this day and age, it sometimes seems as though discipline is a dirty word. Everyone wants to "do his own thing" and "do it *my* way" without restrictions or limitations. However, discipline is at the foundation of life.

The athlete cannot win the race without discipline. Athletes constantly train. They also refrain from harmful practices such as smoking or drugs or overeating or junk food, or any such practice that does not contribute to the goal. The practicing Christian, likewise, chooses to discipline himself to practice and grow in faith. They also refrain from practices that would distract and would not contribute to relationship with the Lord. The journalist does not write random nonsense; the builder does not lay bricks at random; the surgeon does not cut randomly; the bookkeeper does not tabulate figures at random; each depending on whether they feel like it at the time. They all bend their will to a greater purpose and limit their actions suitable for their trade to perform certain, well-defined, well-thought-out procedures in proper sequence to accomplish the goal.

> *"Faith is taking the first step even when you don't see the whole staircase."*
>
> – Martin Luther King, Jr.

Even the artist, the sculptor, and the poet, while they have great artistic freedom, work within their medium and bend their actions to express what is in them in the way in which they have chosen.

In reality, structure is not so much restrictive as it is *freeing*. It frees us from having to reinvent the wheel, from retrying bad practices known not to work, from produce unsafe, unmaintainable, unreadable, unfixable designs. It reduces the extraneous possibilities that we have to consider, leaving only the better choices to focus on. This also makes it easier to accomplish.

For instance, suppose we had 12 items or options (we'll call them nodes). We might think that the best way would be to connect them all together. If all were connected, we'd have 66 connections – from just 12 nodes!

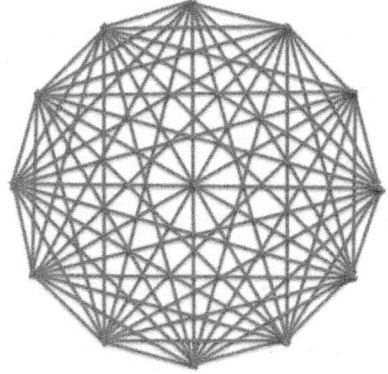

Connectivity, 12 nodes, 66 bi-directional connections

Figure 1 – Connectivity of 12 nodes, 66 connections
(by author)

Unexpectedly complex!

On the other hand, if we limit our options by only connecting what *needs* to be connected, we greatly reduce the complexity. We also increase the efficiency and likely the effectiveness of the result. Suppose these were the only nodes that needed to be connected to each other:

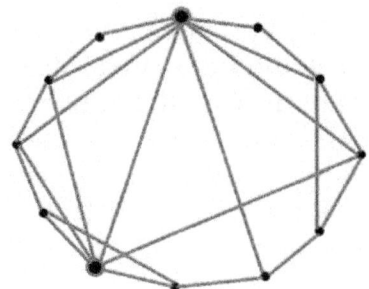

*Figure 2 – "Small world" network example:
12 nodes, 22 connections
(Schulllz, CC BY-SA 3.0, Wikipedia)*

See how removing unneeded options has simplified the situation: Only 23 needed connections remain.

"Form is liberating"

-- Anon.

It is the same with programming. While programming and design are as much arts or crafts as sciences, discipline and structure are still necessary. The programmer[7] and software designer have a plethora of valid design choices, yet retain a great deal of creative freedom. However, they limit themselves to work within certain design paradigms and to utilize certain structures. This allows better, cleaner, easier, and more correctly achieving their end goal – a working program system that does what the client[8] needs. Using only the allowed few structures is instrumental in accomplishing this.

> *The importance of reading actual real-world programs*
>
> As with writing and literature, that we need to learn and grow by actually **reading** other people's program code as often and as much as possible. Preferably, read *well-written, correct* code! Especially include published code (e.g., Jon Bentley's *Programming Pearls*, Henry Ledgard's work, etc.; see "Bibliographical Index"). If available, read real-world extant production programs (as opposed to academic exercises) at your place of employment.

---

[7] Or "coder" or software "developer"; the three terms are synonymous.

[8] If we're writing a program for our own use, then we, ourselves, are the client.

Overall Structure of a Typical Program

"For precept must be upon precept, precept upon precept; line upon line, line upon line; here a little, and there a little."

— *Isaiah 28:10-13* (KJV)

Let us look, then, at the overall structure of a typical program in a generic table of contents-style overview. But first, a brief word about other kinds of non-traditional programming and how they relate to this.

> *Object-oriented programming*
>
> Note that we confine ourselves to "structured" programs and traditional programming, here. <u>Object-oriented</u> (*O-O*) programming is similar at the internal coding level. Our techniques may be used when writing O-O methods, message functions, and related object-oriented code segments. Object-oriented design and higher-level, large-scale design of whole software systems are beyond the scope of this book. They are both larger in scale and broader in scope, and are treated separately within the field of software engineering.
>
> Objects and classes have associated program algorithms (usually called "methods") which internally use the structures and methods discussed here. We can view objects as structures with their associated program methods and data. In some ways, object-oriented programming is more like modeling the problem domain than it is coding computer instructions. (For more, see "class", pp.10 and 97, and "object", p.97, below.)
>
> Detailed object design techniques differ from those in programming just as the bricklayer's tools differ from the architect's.

And still others:

> *Other kinds of non-traditional programming*
>
> There are still other kinds of programming languages — simulation and modeling languages of several types, for instance; graphical and image-processing languages; string and text processing languages; languages for so-called "embedded systems" that run

---

[2] The <u>requirements</u> of a program or system are a statement of what it is expected or required to do, generally expressed in functional or business terms rather than in technical computer terms. It is a major interface documenting the understanding between the client and the developer.

> hardware devices and appliances ranging from refrigerators to army tanks; avionics-oriented languages that run airplanes; languages for artificial intelligence (AI); and many other special-purpose languages. Some of them have similarities to traditional programming and others are strange and unique. None are treated here.

Now let us look at a "table of contents"-style overview of a typical program. This outline is not our guiding light in writing a program – this outline is the *result*, not the cause, of the program design. This outline is dictated by the syntax of the language we are using and of the program-construction algorithm in this book. Like a book, every program is different and will have a different specific table of contents. But generally speaking, the following general plan is typical. A language-specific version will often be presented in the manuals for any given programming language.

Table of Contents (TOC) Outline of a Typical Program

Program ::= [10]

1. Introductory Overview Documentation Block
This should tell what the problem is that the program solves: what the program is all about; any assumptions that go into it; a summary of its input and output data, and perhaps a sketch of how the program goes about solving the problem. It is primarily about the "what" and only secondarily about the "how".

2. External View/Declarations, *as needed*
These may come first, if and only if the programming language demands it; some languages don't require them at all

3. Declarations (Internal)
A layout of the data and variables needed in the program. Other kinds of declarations may also be needed in some languages (see also "Appendix 2 – Variables, data types, and data structures", p.93). In some languages, each declaration can be individually located immediately before its first use in the procedural body, below. In many languages they must be up front as we've placed them here.

4. Initialization Procedure, *as needed*
Procedures to initialize and set-up for the main processing algorithms; most programs will need this.

5. Execution Pre-Conditions and Data Verification Processing, *as needed*

6. **Algorithmic Procedural Body** – the meat of the program
In essence, this is what the rest of this book deals with

7. Cleanup, Closeout, and End-of-Job (EOJ) Processing, *as needed*

8. Subprograms and Subprocedures (internal)
These may come first, if and only if the programming language demands it (see "Subroutines", p.77), otherwise they come last.

Notes:

A separate section of global ("public") data shared by multiple programs in a system is also often included. As it is used and shared by all, it is external and not a component of any of the associated programs, and so is not shown here. Shared data can have its

---

[10] In a lot of notations such as BNF (which is used to define syntax of programming languages, for instance when writing compilers), "::=" means "is defined as". So here, we're saying a program is defined as (or in this case, is composed of) the following elements.

drawbacks as well as its advantages. It can be better to use other techniques such as objects, instead.

Similarly, external subroutines and procedures called by this (and potentially many other) program(s) are not shown here. (More on Subroutines, p. 77 below.) They're separate programs built in the same way and with the same kinds of generic TOC outlines.

Object-oriented programs will also have associated (often separate) sections for local and inherited classes of data.

Fundamental Programming Algorithm

> *"Life is a process: just one thing after another."*
> — Richard Carlson
>
> *"Step by step one goes very far."*
> — Anon.
>
> "Slowly I turn, <u>step by step</u>, inch by inch...."
> — James Barton, Vaudeville actor
> (Also attributed to Moe Howard of the Three Stooges)
> [emphasis added]

After this brief overview, let us now look in more depth at the **process** of developing a program. It is an algorithm of only three steps repeated as often as necessary until the program is complete.

Algorithms

We've used the term several times. Here's a definition. An algorithm is a step-by-step process or procedure for solving a problem or accomplishing the specified goal required of a program. (In other contexts, an algorithm can be a method for solving a mathematical equation.) Computer programs are algorithms coded in a programming language. Algorithms, processes, and procedures detail *how* something is done (as opposed to *what* is to be done).

A <u>heuristic</u>, on the other hand, is a rule of thumb that often will be faster and easier but has no guarantee either of correctness or termination. It might run forever or never get to an answer or an end. It might even produce a result that isn't strictly correct but hopefully is close.

In this section, we discuss a generalized algorithm for how programmers develop computer programs.

This method of programming is a hierarchical, iterative, top-down process. It begins with the initial large-scale functional problem statement as given by the client. This problems statement is expressed in functional (non-computer), problem-oriented – usually business-oriented – terms.

After this point, **the algorithm is simple – divide and conquer**, using the valid control structures. (Note that this algorithm concerns primarily the procedural portions of the program layout as sketched in the "Table of Contents (TOC) Outline of a Typical Program", p.9 above.)

This top-down stepwise process relies on confidence, trust, even faith. We have confidence what we define at a higher level, we will be able to flesh out and detail in the lower levels. (More on this, later.)

Our program-development algorithm is a simple three-step process repeated as necessary. Or ... well, ... maybe it's a four-step process. Let's see:

Step 0 – Think first! Plan ahead!

Don't just jump in blindly. Think first! This is called planning. We need to consider our goal (the business function we need to automate) and ponder how we might achieve that. At worst, this lets us know how to recognize success when we see it: Have we achieved that function? If so, we succeeded. More importantly, it also gives us a feel for where we're going and especially how we might get there – a sketch of our planned actions. We'll have more on this as we go through.

At this point, at the beginning, we start out in functional business terms. What does the client or user want to do with the software? How is it going to work in business? That kind of thing. All about *what*, not *how*. As we break it down and refine its subsequent steps, we get progressively into how to accomplish what is needed.

Advanced programmers will note that we're "programming in the small". We assume that the prior, higher-level, whole-system-oriented steps have already been accomplished. These typically include such things as business process analysis, systems analysis, systems design, and the like. Our *program* planning step, is on a lower level. It deals with what we need to do to address the problem that this particular program is to solve. Beginning programmers at this early stage, need only worry about this central, procedural programming kernel. The rest that encompasses it will come later.

Ater we understand what is needed in user/business terms, one of our first considerations is how to represent it in data and Data structures (p.95). For starters, we need to know the input data and the output data and what they look like. Then consider how to represent that. Only then can we consider how to do the processing that our program will need, and that's our first real step. When using object-oriented programming, this consideration of data and data structures includes the classes and objects that will be needed. As is commonly said, "get the data structure right and the program will write itself". (An overstatement, to be sure, but it gets the point across.)

While we are considering the inputs, outputs, and business function, it is best to also develop, or at least consider, testing criteria. These are test cases that tell us how to recognize success when we've achieved it (and when we haven't). Tests such as: does this input produce the specified output, and so forth. (If it doesn't, then we've got more work to do!) It is important that we also need to note the correct outcome at this point. We'll see if it matches the results when we eventually run the program. If we don't know the right answer, we won't know whether our program is working right. (More on all this as we go through it below.)

Having a plan and a sense of the data, we can now begin our algorithm for writing a procedural program.

Fundamental Programming Algorithm

Step 1 – Begin at the Beginning

We begin with the initial large-scale, functional problem statement as given by the client, expressed in functional, non-computer-oriented terms. Treat it as a "black box" that expresses *what* it does without (yet) knowing *how* it does it. (A "*black box*" is opaque in that we can't see into it. We can only tell what it does, its inputs and outputs. We can't tell *how* it does it. That comes later.)

Step 2 – Divide and Conquer

Break a function down into the subordinate structure that, when executed, performs that function

Select a[11] black box *function*[12] in the expression of the problem or program (e.g., a procedure block on a flowchart). Expand this function by replacing it with the structure[13] that performs that function. That is, expand the functional statement of *what* the function *is* into the procedural structure that shows *how* that function is *performed*. Each resulting subordinate block of the new structure should itself be expressed in functional black box *what*-not-*how* terms.

The "original" functional black box statement should be retained as an explanatory comment describing what the new structure does. (This will help later on in many ways: in checking our work; in understanding the program later on; in eventual program maintenance; and in any validation, correctness-proving, or re-engineering efforts.)

It is important to note that the new structure and the business function *do the same thing* and are merely expressed in different levels of detail. (They're also expressed in

---

[11] While we can validly select *any* black box function to decompose, it's best to select the *next logical* black box function to decompose.

[12] We'll generally use the term "function" to indicate a higher-level functional specification – a *what*. We'll use "process" or "procedure" to indicate a lower-level element that is part of a structure or an algorithm to accomplish the function – part of the *how*. Unfortunately, the term "function" is often used interchangeably for this lower-level process element, as well, since the one elaborates or decomposes into the other. The meaning can be distinguished by the context.

There is also a kind of a subprogram called a Function (see "Subroutine", p. 83) and there is an operation in math called a function. Except in the section on subroutines or when clearly spelled out, the term "function" in this book *never* means either of these. Rather "function", for us, means the high-level statement of something to be done – the "*what*" without yet considering the details of *how* to accomplish it. Again, the meaning can be distinguished by context.

[13] Perhaps we should say "replace it with **a** valid structure" rather than "replace it with **the** structure". There is plenty of room for design choices, engineering trade-offs, and (for the more advanced programmer) even craftsmanship or artistic expression. There are usually several alternative equivalent structures that can perform this same black box function. More on this later.

different languages – the higher-level black box is expressed in human or business or systems analysis language. The lower-level procedure is expressed in the computer programming language or pseudo-code or diagrams.)

Therefore, at any point, we should be able to look at a structure or substructure, see what it does, and be assured that what it is doing is the same thing as the original statement of that function. If it is not equivalent, something has gone wrong. In other words, we can be assured that the program is correct – that it does in fact do what its functional problem statement requires[14]. (This assumes, of course, that we have not made some inadvertent mistake or typo along the way. Humans do, after all, make mistakes.)

At all points in the development process, we have a *complete* and correct program (albeit with varying levels of detail). Some, un-expanded higher-level portions may still be expressed in broad, functional, problem-oriented terms saying *what* is to be done. Other portions may be expressed in specific, detailed, lower-level, more computer-oriented, terms saying *how* to do it. If we were to "zoom out" and take a bird's eye view of the program, we could see these differing levels of detail. Yet we would see an entire program consistent with the original problem statement.

We can think of this like an artist painting a canvas. The artist may make a rough sketch of the entire painting on the canvas. Gradually add shapes, colors, areas, and details. We may go rather broadly over the canvas one phase at a time, refining the result. At any given point, an entire picture might be viewed. However, differing areas will have different degrees of completion at different times.

We can contrast this approach to other methods of program composition that are more like constructing a building brick-by-brick. With that approach, one portion is completed but another is merely planned. The entire structure is not visible until the very end when, at last, it is *all* completed.

Graphically, Step 2 of the algorithm can be diagrammed like this:

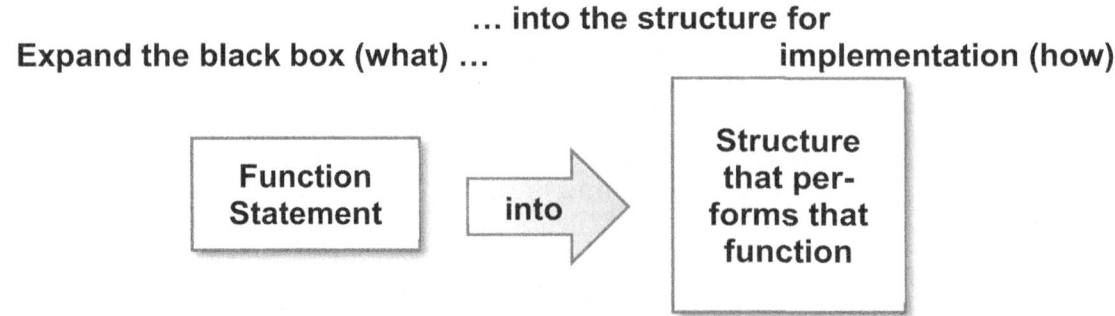

---

[14] The industry is indebted to Harlan Mills for proving that this structured, top-down, divide-and-conquer approach is identical to producing a mathematical proof of correctness. This is a blessing, as it assures us that our program is correct without going through the pain of a formal, mathematical, proof. That assumes that we use these methods, of course. For details, see his paper, "How to write correct programs and know it" in *Proc. 1975 International Conference on Reliable Software*, listed in the Bibliographical Index on pp.137ff, below.

Fundamental Programming Algorithm

Step 3 – Lather, Rinse, Repeat

Recurse[15] or Repeat

Repeat until done. Repeat *Step 2*, function by function, block by block, repetitively replacing each function with procedural structures that perform the function. Expand newly-created subordinate functions also. Continue until we reach the level of the low-level programming "primitives" in our programming language (i.e., the programming language statements or commands themselves). When the entire program is expressed in programming language statements, the process is complete.

Lastly, Trust (or not) but Verify

Well, actually, *don't* trust – *test* and verify.

"The best laid schemes o' Mice an' Men
Gang aft agley"

Translation from Scots dialect:
"The best laid plans of mice and men
often go awry."

-- Robert Burns, "To a mouse", 1785

"Testing shows the presence, not the absence, of bugs."

-- Edsger W. Dijkstra, during panel discussion
at NATO 1969 Conference on Software
Engineering Techniques

Because we're only human, we always need to test and verify. It is best to develop the testing criteria at the beginning, during planning (see above). Testing is a huge subject in its own right and will not be considered in detail here. However, two kinds of testing must be mentioned:

1. First, during the development process of breaking down each function into subordinate structures during program development: Ask ourselves at each step whether our new structure in fact accomplishes the function being detailed. If not, we've selected the wrong structure or the wrong parameters. Knowing this is critical to

---

[15] Briefly, *Recursion* is a form of repetition in which a thing calls or invokes itself. Some programming languages allow recursion, though it is beyond the scope of this book. Here, all we mean is to repeat the same top-down decomposition program-creation algorithm until done.

correctness and success. Such structural questions are presented below as we explain each structure.

2. Later, when the program is a "completed first draft": Test-run the software itself (based on the test criteria and test cases we develop at in the planning stage). This is what tells us when (and whether) we've achieved success. There are at least two general areas of software testing that I'll very loosely group into unit testing and integration testing.

    o *Unit testing* tests each of the separate pieces of the software and can be done alone as we go along, as long as there's a completed unit or subunit to test.

    o *Integration testing* tests the whole assembly of programs of pieces. It comes in many varieties and is done when we've completed the program (or enough that it has pieces that need to be tested together). This can be extensive and in many layers and tiers. It is so extensive that it takes books to cover adequately, and will not be further detailed in this book. When starting out, "just do it" – do the best you can with testing, learn while doing, and read up on it elsewhere as necessary.

If we've done everything correctly and according to this process as we go along, then the tests should pass easily and without much anguish. If not, they should point us in the direction of what to fix. (A bit more on *that*, in "Appendix 5 – A word on program maintenance and debugging", p. 123, below.)

As Steve McConnell notes in *Code Complete*, "Testing's goal runs counter to the goals of other development activities. The goal is to *find* errors. A successful test is one that breaks the software. The goal of every other development activity is to *prevent* errors and keep the software from breaking." [emphasis added]

One final note: It may be useful to briefly scan "Appendix 7 – A brief introduction to systems analysis" (p.137). Although systems analysis is at a higher level than programming, the similarities of the processes can also illuminate our programming methods, here.

The programming process should look something like this:

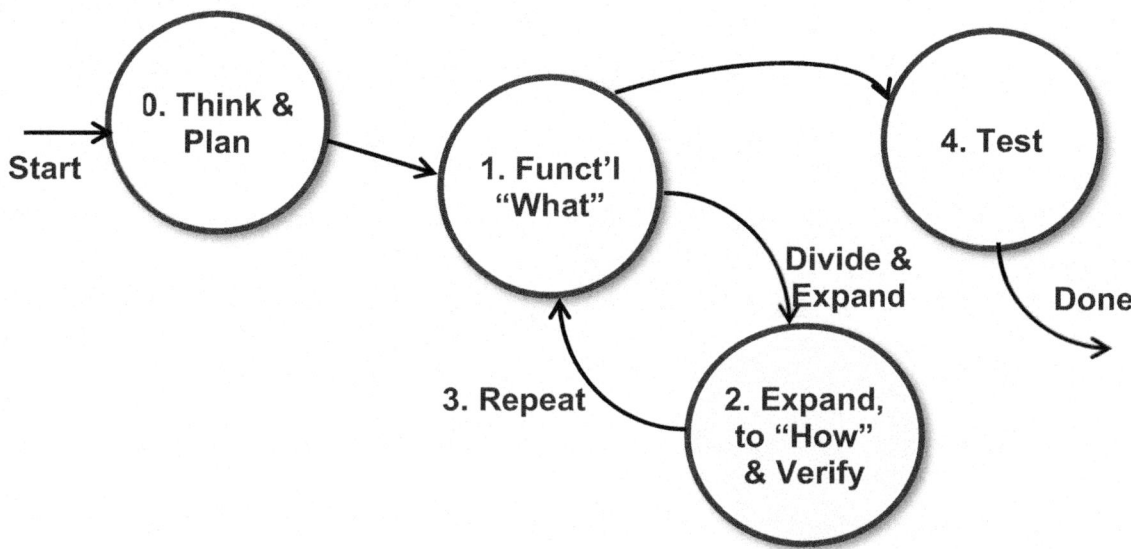

Figure 3 - Fundamental Programming Algorithm

The core of programming, then, is Step 2 – Divide and Conquer. How to do that is next.

On Programming

Fundamental Structure Theorem

> *"... when a designer does not understand a problem clearly enough to find the order it really calls for[16], he falls back on some arbitrarily chosen formal order. The problem, because of its complexity, remains unsolved."*
>
> – Christopher Alexander, *Notes on the Synthesis of Form*, 1964

The expansion of function `F` into the structure that performs function `F` (symbolically, `F → Structure(F)`) is important. It links the functional, top-down, goal-directed nature of programming (see above) with the actual programming structures that perform these functions.

Now, as the Structure Theorem below shows, this is the key because anything that can be programmed, can be programmed (and programmed *better*) using the correct structures. We don't need to add anything else. This is one of the major factors that both lends discipline to programming and also creates discipline and structure to the resulting programs. For that reason, it is also one of the major factors increasing readability and maintainability. For reasons beyond the scope of this book (see Harlan Mills' works in "Bibliographical Index"), it also adds mathematical rigor and is one of the few things that ensures correctness in the programmed product, when followed up with the verification questions for each structure discussed below.

The *Fundamental Structure Theorem* of Structured Programming[17], then, is that it has been proven that:

Fundamental Structure Theorem

All programs that can be flowcharted (which is essentially all programs), can be programmed using only the following three control structures: **Sequence**, **If-Then-Else**, *and* **Do-While**.

That does not mean that we must be limited to only these three. We will present a few more equivalent structures that can be derived from these three. However, when we need to do so, we can program using only **Sequence**, **If-Then-Else**, and **While**. In fact, for correctness of our programs, we actually *do* need to limit it to only these three (plus the very few valid equivalents given later, below).

---

[16] In our context, Alexander's "order it really calls for" is the few structures presented herein.

[17] See *Structured programming – theory and practice* by Richard Linger, Harlan Mills, and Bernard Witt and "How to write correct programs and know it" by Harlan Mills, both referenced in the Bibliographical Index on pp.137ff.

In any case, it is necessary to limit ourselves to a valid subset of structures. Unfortunately, much that is flowchartable and programmable is spaghetti code. Such programs are either not valid, their correctness is not verifiable, or they are so complex that even if they were verifiable, they would still be intractable messes. Therefore, only the structures discussed here should be used. Indeed, beginners should further limit themselves to only the "big three" until they gain the experience to know when they can validly use the others (and when they cannot).

Three fundamental structures and how to use them

> *"Since large programs grow from small ones, it is crucial that we develop an arsenal of standard program structures of whose correctness we have become sure—we call them idioms—and learn to combine them into larger structures using organizational techniques of proven value."*
>
> — Alan J. Perlis, as quoted in Structure and Interpretation of Computer Programs

Three basic structures

So, what are these structures? Let's finally discuss these basic building blocks, the programming structures themselves. For each, we will include:

- an example,
- the *pseudo-code*[18] statements comprising the structure,
- the flowchart of the structure,
- the Nassi-Schneiderman Chart[19] (or *N-S Chart*) of the structure, and
- the data-flow chart (or *data flow diagram*, *DFD*) of the structure[20].

We will also give an extended example, building a short program piece-by-piece throughout this book as we examine the major control structures.

Why include all these charts? First, because we see each of them in different contexts at different times and we should be familiar with what they are. Second, because they each have different fortes and somewhat different uses. Third, because people learn

---

[18] We use an informal, generalized programming-like *pseudo-code* so that we are not tied to just a single programming language. Pseudo-code cannot be translated by a compiler and cannot be executed by a computer. But it is clearer, higher level, and more generalized for its human-only audience. We use it to make what amounts to sketches of programs before proceeding to writing a formal program in a specific programming language. (All such real programming languages, unlike pseudo-code, have rigid syntax and other conventions.) Do pseudo-code by hand in pencil on paper or on chalkboards or whiteboards. Typing it gives the impression that it's more forma and that it is another programming language, which it isn't.

[19] Also called a *Chapin Chart*. More below, in "A note on *Nassi-Schneiderman Charts*".

[20] We do not include a separate dictionary or glossary of notation for the various charts. Such information can be had elsewhere. Instead, we will explain both the charts and some points of notation in context as we go along. Note also that there are several different types and formats of data-flow diagrams for different purposes, of which we are using only one.

differently and are comfortable with different presentations and points of view. Some like it graphical, some like textual, etc. So, all are presented so that everyone may better grasp the concepts presented.

Should all programs be flowcharted? *Of course not!* Nor should all have an N-S chart. Should all have a DFD? *No!* Like hammer, screwdriver, and saw, they are tools for a purpose. We use the ones that are most useful to us in the context in which we need them. Remember the others for use in another context, when needed. The important thing is the programming methods and structures themselves, not the notation they are presented in.

Think first! Plan ahead! As Dave Thomas and Andrew Hunt put it in *The Pragmatic Programmer*, "Proceed from a plan, whether that plan is in your head, on the back of a cocktail napkin, or on a whiteboard". Or as here, in an appropriate diagram of some sort.

In addition to the structures, we will also discuss verification questions we should ask ourselves when checking the program. For each structure, ask the corresponding questions for that structure to verify that it is correct.[21]

The three fundamental structures, then, are:

- `Sequence`,
- `If-Then-Else`, and
- `Do-While`.

Three additional valid structures derived from these three are `Repeat-Until`, `Select-Case`, and `For-Loop`, which are described later.

Significantly, **all valid structures have exactly one entry point and one exit point**. This can best be seen by contrasting with invalid, Unsafe Structures (p. 79).

Detailed discussion of the fundamental program structures[22] follows.

---

[21] Here, we express these correctness verification questions in English prose, rather than in the predicate calculus logic that the originators used. Ours is a pragmatic practitioner's guide to programming rather than a rigorous theoretical text.

[22] Essentially all modern programming languages have all these structures and more besides. In the rare cases where they aren't built-in, the structures should still be used. However, they will have to be built "by hand" from lower-level statements such as `GO-TO` (which, other than this, should be avoided).

Sequence

> *And now the sequence of events in no particular order.*
> – Dan Rather

> *"For the great doesn't happen through impulse alone, and is a succession of little things that are brought together."*
> – Vincent van Gogh, letter to his brother Theo, 1882

Use **Sequence** when function F is accomplished by first doing one thing or part (say, A) followed by then doing another part (say B):

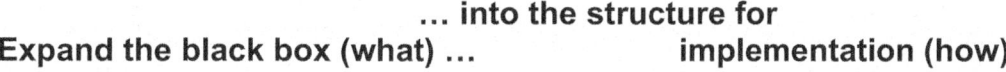

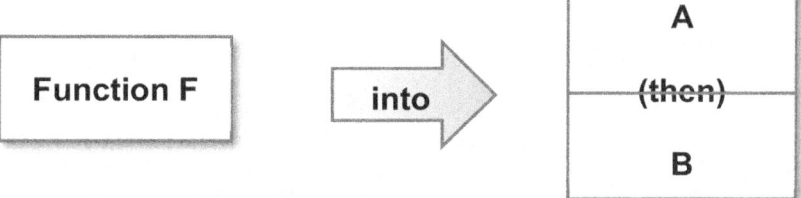

Note: This can be extended and daisy chained as far as necessary. In other words, this (though possibly a bit harder to self-check or validate) is also **Sequence**:

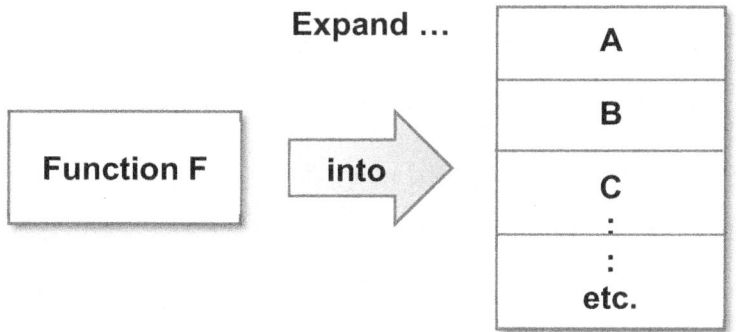

When to use the Sequence structure

Choose the **Sequence** structure when we need to do several things in order, or when we need to do several things whose order doesn't matter (more on this below).

Sequence Example – eating

Let's take a classic (and actual) example from *Sesame Street*. Cookie Monster asks, "should I open my mouth *before* I eat the cookie or *after* I eat the cookie?" If our function F is the whole process of eating the cookie, then we open our mouth (A) before we chew the cookie (B). So F is done by doing A then B in sequential order. Doing B then A would *not* do F; we could not chew the cookie before opening our mouth!

Sequence Pseudo-code

```
A;

B;
```

Or in some computer languages and pseudo-code notations:

```
Begin
    A;
    B;
End
```

Note:

In some pseudo-code notations and some programming languages, keywords like **Begin** and **End** are boldfaced or even colorized to distinguish from variables.

Similarly, in some pseudo-code and some programming languages, statements (commands) end with a semicolon, and in some they do not. We'll use them hereafter as statement separators where it helps clarify and will omit them otherwise.

Either way it's shown, what it's saying is that our original function F is performed by first doing A (whatever that may be) followed by then doing B.

> Where there's no ambiguity, **Begin** and **End** can be omitted, as can the semicolons. Some pseudo-code notations and some programming languages use **Do** instead of **Begin**, and some require semicolons even after those keywords. Of the notations using **Do**, some end with **End Do**, some end with just **End**, and some with **Od** (which is "do" spelled backwards). Some delimit such blocks with curly braces { and } and there are even some languages that use simple parentheses (and), though that can quickly lead to ambiguity.
>
> Don't let the jargon throw you. They're all equivalent. Here, we'll use the simplest clear notation (usually either **Begin** and **End** or no block delimiters at all). Such simplicity and generality are the beauty of pseudo-code (though no *compiler*[23] can use it directly).
>
> When using pseudo-code, we can use pretty much whatever notation conventions work for us and help clarify.

---

[23] A compiler is the software that translates the programming language statements into the hardware's zeroes and ones, which are the only thing that the hardware can actually execute.

Sequence

Sequence Flowchart

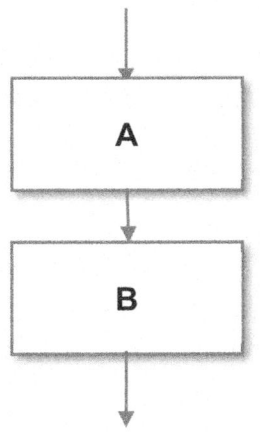

Note:

In a flowchart, lines show flow of control (instruction sequencing). When they go from top to bottom or left to right, we don't usually show the arrowheads. (However, we'll always show them here, for clarity.)

Rectangular boxes indicate processing functions.

Sequence Nassi-Schneiderman Chart (AKA Chapin Chart)

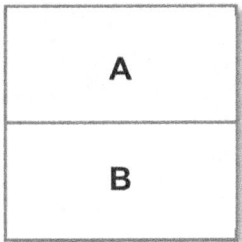

Both the above charts show that F is done by first doing A then doing B.

When A must be done before B (e.g., when A's output is needed as B's input), we put them in connected boxes as above. If it doesn't matter whether A or B is done first, we usually put them both in a single box, like this:

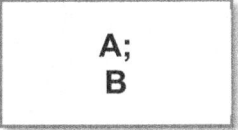

If there's no sub-structure to the parts, we sometimes (perhaps sloppily) use this single-box notation for either situation. We distinguish the meaning by the context.

A note on Nassi-Schneiderman Charts

Part of the beauty of the Nassi-Schneiderman charts is that it's easy to see that the structures just snap together like Lego® blocks. All structures combine like this but it's easiest to see with the Nassi-Schneiderman charts.

The main advantage of N-S Charts, in my view, is that it's actually *impossible* to produce invalid structures or spaghetti code.

Sequence Data Flow Diagram (DFD)

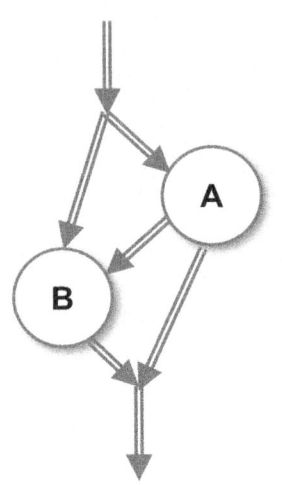

> Note:
>
> In a DFD, lines show flow of data and are generally curved. (As in a flowchart, when they go from top to bottom or left to right, we don't usually show the arrowheads. Again, we'll do so here for clarity.)
>
> When control flow and data flow are combined on the same diagram, the data lines are shown differently (double, dashed, bold, etc.) to avoid confusion. Here, we'll use double lines for data flow.
>
> Round bubbles indicate processing functions and conditions. They're equivalent to flowcharts' rectangular and diamond boxes.

This chart shows that:

- both A and B (may) use the input data; and
- B uses for input data what A provides as output data (which is why B is second, not A); and
- both A and B contribute to the final output of the structure.[24]

Sequence Verification Check

To check our work, we ask ourselves: Does doing A then doing B accomplish F? Or, what does doing A then doing B do? Is it F, that it does? If so, the sequence structure is correct.

Using the Cookie Monster example, does opening our mouth then chewing eat the cookie? Yes. Or what does opening our mouth then chewing do? Eat the cookie! So, it works, it's correct.

---

[24] In many cases only A uses the input data (and B doesn't), and B uses only A's output data (not the input data), and only B (not A) produces the (only) output result of the structure. It's like a daisy chain or waterfall. As the above comment shows, however, it can sometimes be more complicated than that.

Extended Example – ACL access

Let's take work on an extended example and build it piece-by-piece as we go through the structures. We'll start by filling in information from the Table of Contents (TOC) Outline of a Typical Program (see p.9).

Problem statement

Our extended example's purpose (the initial "function F", as we've been calling it) is to determine whether or not to authorize the computer user to access a specified data file. Specifically, we will compare the User ID to an Access Control List (ACL) of files and their authorized users. Remember this, as we'll use it below.

Input

In order for this to work, we will need to

- know which file the user wants to access (we'll call this the data file),
- get the user's User ID, and
- read the master ACL file.

So, our inputs will be the File ID, ACL master file name, and User ID.

The ACL master file is a built-in operating system file which lists all files and all user IDs permitted to access each one (or alternatively, all user IDs and all files each user is permitted to access). So, we will get our answer by searching to see whether our particular user-requested data file and User ID are listed in the ACL master file as being permitted.

(In a real situation, the ACL would most likely be a database (DB), not a simple file, and we'd access it via calls to routines in a database management system (DBMS). That's way beyond the scope of this book, however the program's structure would be the same. We'd just use DBMS calls instead of the file *reads* that we'll see here.)

Output

We have only a single logical (Boolean) output result: `True` if access is to be granted, and `False` if it is not. We don't have to read the data file the user is requesting; that's some other program's job. In fact, that other program will call this extended example program first to unlock and get the go-ahead (`true` or `false`) to read the data file, and then will access the data file by itself. So if our resulting output is `false`, then that program will display a reject message to the user and will quit. If our result is `true`, then that calling program will open and read the data file that the user wants.

Program outline

Introductory Overview Documentation Block

Here, we'd copy in something like

- the Problem Statement paragraph, and
- the first section of the second (Input) paragraph, and

On Programming

- the first sentence of the third (Output) paragraph, above.

When we get to the stage of coding the program into a specific programming language, we'd make these into comments (see "Comments in programming", p.30). We probably wouldn't include this in pseudo-code, however. Rather, we'd probably just let the above narrative problem statement suffice. (If we're in a programming course, this would be given to us by the instructor or problem statement and we wouldn't have to do *anything* with it.) One way or another, this information would be provided either to us or by us.

External View/Declarations, as needed

There are none in this simplistic problem (and none in charting). In a real program, this would be required in the program code. But that's language- and operating system-dependent and is beyond the scope of this book.

Internal Declarations

Pseudo-code is at too high a level to need or use any *declarations*[25]. (There also are no declarations in charting, as charts are procedure oriented, and declarations are primarily data-oriented.) Once we code this into a specific programming language, however, our declarations might look something like this (likely with additional information about each):

Define Result as Boolean

Define Data_File_ID as String

Define ACL_File_ID as String

Define User_ID as String

> As always, the format of data definitions and declarations varies with each programming language. **Dim**, or **Dimension**, or sometimes **Def**, for instance, are common keywords for where I've used **Define**. Some programming languages are "typeless" and all the data definitions and conversions are handled automatically and don't need explicit definition. That's convenient and makes it easy. But it has a downside, too. Advantages include clearly specifying exactly what variables (and functions and subprograms) we are using, exactly what their type and format is, adding a comment as to their usage and meaning, and so forth. Among other things, the compiler can then enforce it and make sure we don't mess things up by inappropriately using them.

---

[25] See "Data types", p.93.

Sequence

Initialization procedure and initialization for the main processing algorithms

Initialization is the first major block of most programs. It includes getting the input data, opening any files (e.g., the ACL), and general setting-up. Actually, opening the files must come after first finding the file names, verifying the their existence, etc. So we'll use a *sequence*:

> **Get Data File ID**
> **Get ACL File ID**
> **Get User ID**
>
> **Open ACL File**

Execution Pre-Conditions and Data Verification Processing,

This is primarily to screen out and reject invalid input data. For instance, in the current example program, perhaps the user doesn't tell us what data file he or she wants to access. Or perhaps we see that it includes invalid data (e.g., typos). Or maybe the data file doesn't even exist. In our ACL case, we'd have to validate the filename *before* we open it. In most non-input/output situations, we'd do the initialization setup (above) before we verify preconditions and parameters. That's why it's normally second in our programming procedure.

> **Validate Data File ID**

Algorithmic Procedural Body – the meat of the program

Here's the meat of our program:

> **Determine whether User ID is listed in ACL record for Data File**

Cleanup, Closeout, and End-of-Job (EOJ) Processing, as needed

What do we do when we've accomplished it? Output or return the result, close any open files, and general clean up.

> **Close Files**
> **Return Result**
> **(true/false)**

Subprograms and Subprocedures

None in our simple example.

On Programming

Sequence of whole program

So, here's the resulting Nassi-Schneiderman chart of our example, so far:

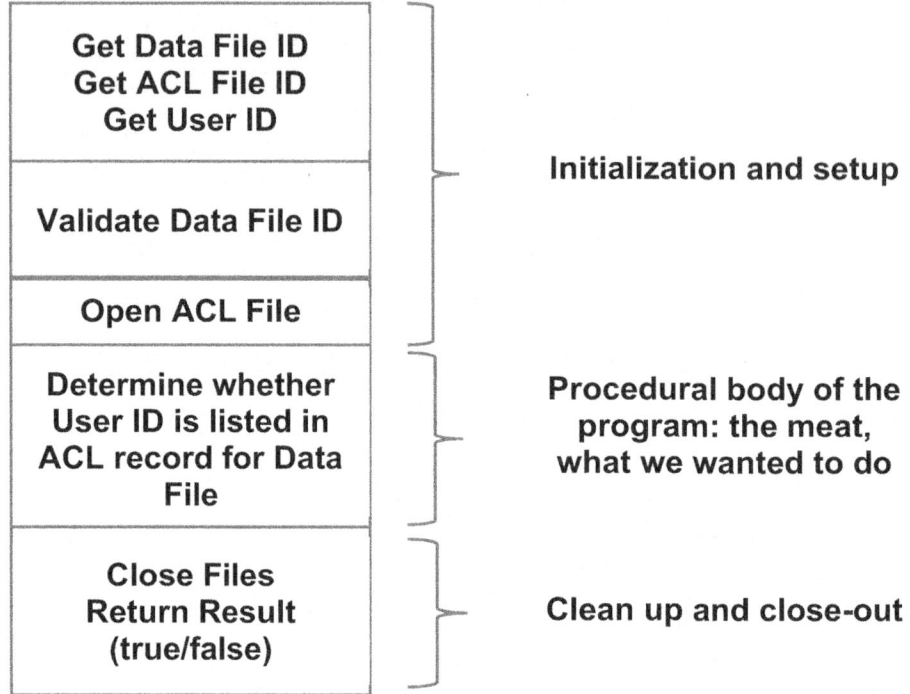

Note that that's a complete program and accomplishes the entire problem statement. It isn't very detailed, but at this stage that's fine. We'll flesh it out and expand it as we go.

Almost all programs have this three-part structure:

1) Initialization and setup,
2) procedural body, and
3) clean-up and close-out.

Object-oriented programs do some of this in the classes and some in the methods, but these pieces are necessary for pretty much any program to work.

Comments in programming

As we go, I'll mention several areas in which various programming languages and pseudo-code notations use different syntaxes for keywords, structures, commands, and the like. We've already seen block structure differences, for instance (**Begin** and **End**, **Do** and **End-Do**, semicolon statement separators (or not), etc.). Here is another: Comments.

Comments are remarks inserted in programs for notes and documentation. They are ignored by the compiler and not executed by the computer. They are purely for the programmer and for subsequent debuggers, enhancers, and maintainers. Different programming languages use a wide variety of different conventions for comments. Common notations are beginning a comment with a single quote (' or '), an asterisk (*), two slashes

(**//**), two dashes (**--**), two colons (**::**), a number-sign or hash-mark (**#**), and an exclamation point (**!**). Also common are use of paired symbols to begin and end the comment, much like parentheses: **/*** and ***/**, **<<** and **>>**, curly braces **{** and **}**, and so forth.

In pseudo-code we can use any convention that's helpful – as long as we're consistent and don't confuse it with other symbols or notations. In pseudo-code, I usually use either curly braces **{** and **}** or, as I do in this book, square brackets **[** and **]**.

While we're jumping ahead here a little, it's essential to mention that **comments are vital** to programming, debugging, and maintenance. In my experience, the most critical comments are an explanation at the beginning of every major block of program code and/or every major program structure. This block comment will tell what that specific code section does or is trying to do. Of course, this doesn't mean that the introductory comment to an **If-Then-Else** structure (for example) should say, "this is an If-Then-Else" structure! Rather, it should tell *in functional terms* what the structure or code block is trying to accomplish. In short, when we expand Function **F** into a block of code, the comment should be the original statement of Function **F**. For example, if the function of this block of code is to read and process the ACL, then the comment should say "read and process ACL". Following that comment, the program code itself should be the detailed statements that actually *do* read and process the ACL.

On Programming

If-Then-Else (Conditional Execution)

> *"Choice means saying no to one thing so you can say yes to another."*
> – Dan Millman
>
> *"It's choice – not chance – that determines your destiny."*
> – Jean Nidetch
>
> *"May your choices reflect your hopes not your fears."*
> – Nelson Mandela

The **If-Then-Else** structure is about choice. We *choose* one of two or more ways of doing something, or we *choose* which method to use based on the given conditions.

Use **If-Then-Else** (AKA "conditional execution" or "alternation"[26]) when the way that function F is performed depends on some pre-condition. Let's call the condition P. If P is true then doing A accomplishes F, and if P is false then doing B accomplishes F. Or, more precisely in both cases, doing A (or B) does F, *all* of F, *only* F, and *nothing but* F.

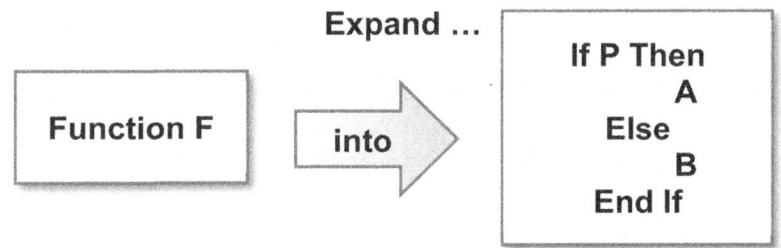

When to use the If-Then-Else structure

Choose the `If-Then-Else` structure when we need to decide upon a choice between alternatives (or between alternative methods for doing something).

If-Then-Else Example – driving routes

Suppose we can get to the airport by either of two routes. We could go through the city (which is shorter in distance but congested). Or we could take the bypass (which is longer but may have less traffic). Then we can say that we get to the airport (F) by considering the traffic conditions. If it's rush hour (P) then we take the bypass around the

---

[26] as in "alternatives"

city (**A**). If it's not rush hour (not **P**, sometimes symbolized as ¬P or P̄ [27] or even !P) then we go directly through the city (**B**). If **P**, then **A** does **F**; otherwise, if **not** **P** then **B** does **F**. That is, if it's rush hour then taking the bypass gets us to the airport best, and if it's not rush hour then going directly through the city gets us to the airport best.

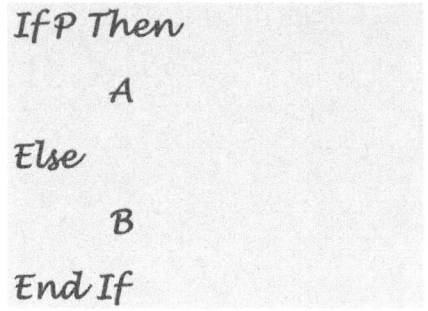

If-Then-Else Pseudo-code

If P Then
    A
Else
    B
End If

Note:

In some pseudo-code notations and almost all programming languages, the **If-Then-Else** structure terminates with **End** or **End If**. In other pseudo-code notations, it just terminates without an ending delimiter (which could seem less clear).

In most formatting schemes, the **Then** keyword is on the same line as the **If**, in some on the same line as **A**, and in a few on its own line. Do it however it's clearest and makes the most sense to you unless your programming language or employer's conventions require otherwise.

Note that in programming, clear and consistent *indentation* of program code is of vital importance. The computer itself couldn't care less. But it makes a big difference to the programmer – especially during follow-on maintenance months or years later. The programmer must understand what the code does in order to write and maintain it correctly. So proper indentation helps. This is nowhere more obvious than in pseudo-code. Yet it is even more important in writing actual programming language source code. We will not go into specific conventions for indenting as there are many alternative conventions. We pick the one that makes the most sense to us personally and with which we are most comfortable[28]. (Or if our employer has coding standards, then we use those.) The point is that indentation exists to make the code more readable and to reflect the structure of the program. If it does not do that, it's not doing its job and we should adopt a better convention.

Remember: Form follows (is determined by) function and this should be reflected in our indentation.

---

[27] Though P̄ is only for pseudo-code and similar notations since the over-score doesn't work in the character sets of programming languages. In this book we use ¬P and **Not P** (and occasionally even **Not-P**) interchangeably.

[28] There are rare exceptions in some programming languages like Python for which indentation is significant and is the only indication to the compiler (i.e., not keywords) of what the block structure is. In such cases, we must indent the way the compiler requires. For the vast majority of cases, however, we indent in whatever way is most clear to us, the programmer.

If-Then-Else (Conditional Execution)

> As above, some languages and notations punctuate with semicolons after the **Else** and the **End** and some do not. Some end with **End If** or even **End-If**, some with just **End**, and some with **Fi** (which is "if" spelled backwards). Some end when the indentation ends, and a few simply end without a keyword.

If-Then-Else Flowchart

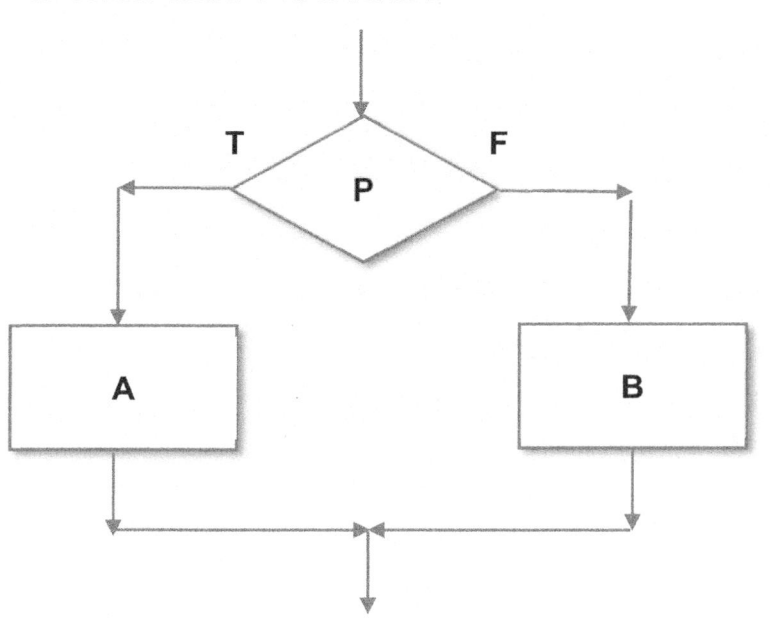

> Note:
>
> A diamond box indicates a True/False (or Yes/No) condition (**P**).
>
> Lines on flowcharts are usually drawn at right angles. They flow top-to-bottom and left-to-right unless noted.
>
> Where two flow lines join (as at the bottom, here) a small circle is sometimes used as a junction. (However, we have not done so herein.)

It is most important to connect the outbound flowlines at the bottom! That's part of what makes this a structure rather than spaghetti code!

"Every choice you make has an end result."

– Zig Ziglar

We can draw the true and false exits from the diamond in the flowchart on either side, as long as we also switch the processing boxes **A** and **B** (see chart above).

Incidentally, "`If P Then A Else B`" is equivalent to "`If (Not P) then B Else A`".

If we don't need it, the **Else B** clause may be omitted. This is equivalent to saying, `If P then A; else do nothing`. In this case, **B** is null. This degenerate case is very common. Here is its flowchart and its alternative:

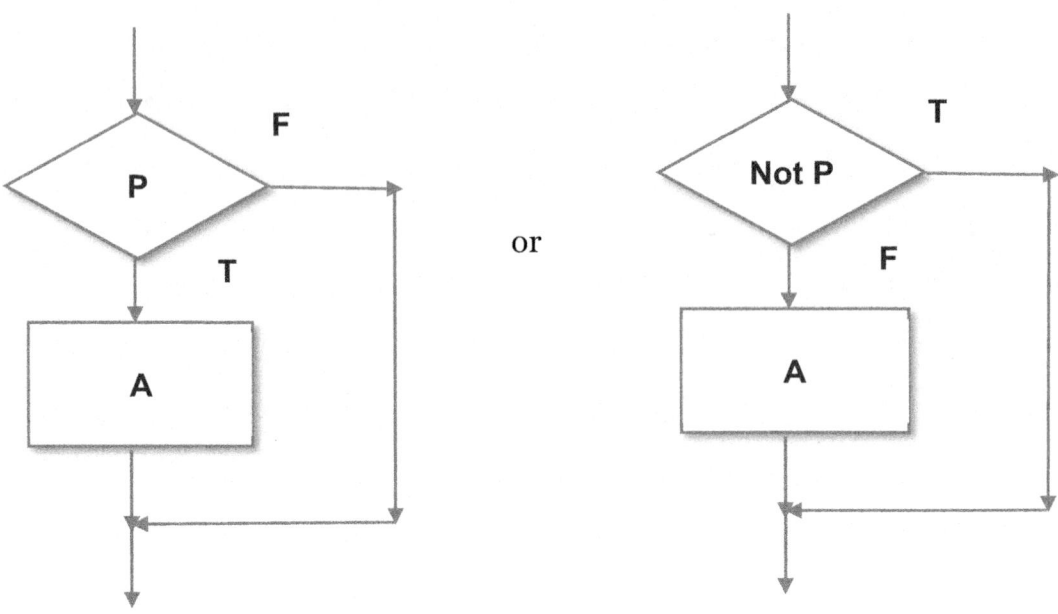

A note about notation

Until now, we've been using letters **F**, **A**, and **B** as functions or (sub-)processes that *do* something. In general, they represent blocks of program code or sub-structures. That is, in a real program, they wouldn't be letters, they'd be blocks of code.

P, on the other hand, represents an *expression*. In this case, it's a logical or true/false expression (AKA a *Boolean* expression). It is like a mathematical formula that evaluates to either true or false. For example, **P** could be "**X < 7**" in the statement "**If X < 7 then print "it's lower"**". Either **X** is less than 7 (in which case, **P** is true) or **X** is not less than 7 (and **P** is false).

The logical condition **P** in an **If** statement is often a comparison like *less than*. It can also be a comparison like *equals*, e.g., "**If X = 7**" means to determine whether (true) or not (false) **X** is 7. Simple enough. This is not an assignment statement (see below). However, in some programming languages the equal sign is used in both assignments (in place of our left arrow "←") and in equality testing in **If** statements, as here. The context determines the difference. So to distinguish them more clearly, some languages use "**:=**" for assignment. Other languages use two equals signs, "**==**", or "**EQU**" to test equality in an **If** statement.

Other expressions can be mathematical as in "**(A * A) + (2 * B * B)**". Text and string expressions are also possible.

Assignments and Variables

Assignment statements assign a value (an expression) to a variable. In programming, a *variable* is much like a variable in math: it is a letter or a name that stands for something and has a value. A variable in programming is the address (like a street address) of

If-Then-Else (Conditional Execution)

a storage location in which we store a value. Or a named pigeon-hole in a wall of mailboxes (see the picture in "arrays", p.94).

So, an assignment statement like "X ← 2 * 3" would calculate the value of 2 times 3 and store the value 6 in the variable named X. We could read this as "Assign 2 times 3 to variable X", "multiply 2 times 3 and store in variable X", or simply "X gets 2 times 3". Think of it any way that makes sense to you.

As noted, in most programming languages, the equal sign (=) is used for assignment, although some use := . On the other hand, in pseudo-code I use a left-pointing arrow, which unfortunately doesn't exist on keyboards. Similarly, programming languages use an asterisk (*) for multiplication because an x would be too easily confused with a variable named X.

If your programming language uses the equal sign for assignment, it's probably best *not* to read "X = 2 * 3" as "X equals 2 times 3". That's too easy to confuse with other things. For instance, don't confuse it with the condition (P) in a statement like If X = 2 * 3 then do something. The condition there is a *test* to see whether or not X actually is 2 * 3 or not. But the assignment *sets* X to 2 * 3. It *makes* X have the value 2 * 3.

Unlike in math, variables don't have to be single letters. So, Pi could be a variable (especially if we had assigned Pi ← 3.14159265) and PAY_RATE and Last_Name could be variables. Later, in examples below, we'll use other letters and names like I, N, N1, N2, etc. as variables.

Assignments are not equations

Incidentally, in math, "X = X + 1" would be problematic to say the least, but not in a programming language. In math, that would be equivalent to saying "0 = 1", which is an oxymoron, a contradiction in terms[29]. Impossible. But an assignment statement isn't an equation. Unlike math, we're not claiming that X is equal to X+1. Rather, we're instructing the computer to add one to X (the right hand-side) then store the result into the variable named X (the left-hand side). That's why the left-arrow ("←") used in pseudo-code is clearer than the equal sign used in programming languages[30]. But for historical reasons, there is no left-arrow character on keyboards, so they had to come up with another notation. Most languages chose the equal sign. So, in programming

---

[29] In algebra, we can modify an equation by doing the same thing to both sides. So if we subtract X from both sides, we get "X − X = X + 1 − X". Since X − X equals 0, that equation simplifies to "0 = 1", which of course is nonsensical.

[30] Note for the advanced: Some programming languages conceive of assignment as pointers. So "X = 2 * 3" would mean X is a pointer to the value that is the result of multiplying 2 times 3. In such languages, the pseudo-code might be written as "X → 2 * 3". That can also be confusing when we get to linked list Data structures, which have pointers from one cell or node to another. This is a very different thing from assignment. If you're one of the people whom it helps you to think of assignments as pointers instead of data movement, you're welcome! If not (personally, it doesn't do anything for me!), then just ignore it and use the left arrow pseudo-code as I do.

languages, the assignment statement "X = X + 1" makes sense and simply means to increment X by 1.

Note that some languages use the operator "++" to mean increment. So, the statement "X++" means "X ← X + 1" and "X++5" means "X ← X + 5".

Here, we'll continue to use P and Q as logical/Boolean expressions and F, A, B, C, D as functions or subprocesses.

If-Then-Else Nassi-Schneiderman (N-S) Chart

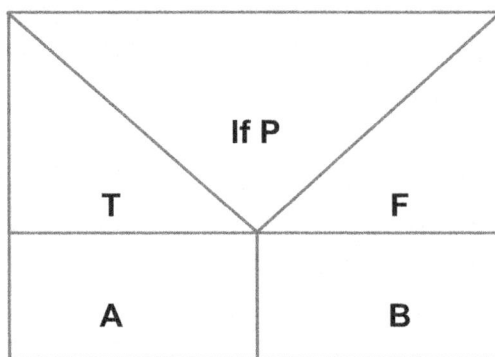

Note:

Control flow in N-S charts is shown by stacking boxes. We stack top-to-bottom for sequence. We stack left-to-right for conditional alternation (as here), and for iteration (later below). We imbed or nest smaller boxes within larger boxes to replace them with more detailed implementing structures. N-S charts do not use flowlines.

As noted above, they snap together like Lego® blocks. A larger Lego block can be replaced by multiple smaller blocks that stack up to the same size and shape. Similarly, an N-S block can be replaced by an N-S structure that does the same thing, as we'll see later.

(N-S structures can also nest within encompassing N-S structures. We'll get to "Nesting structures" below, too.)

Both the flowchart and the N-S chart above show that if P is true, then F is done by doing A, and if P is false then F is done by doing B; and that's all there is to it.

If-Then-Else (Conditional Execution)

If-Then-Else Data Flow Diagram

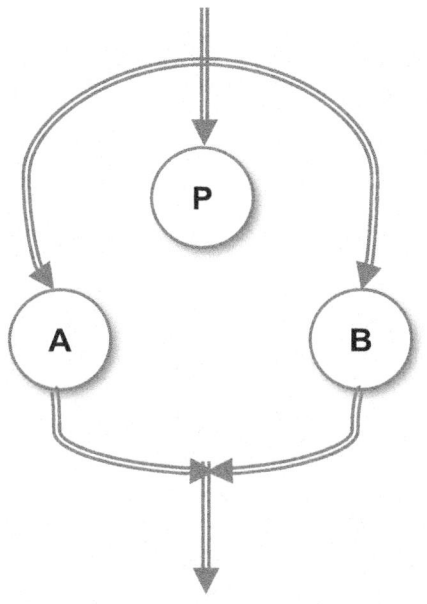

> Note:
>
> Unlike flowcharts, in a DFD, data flow lines are usually drawn as curved arcs. (I sometimes find curves harder to draw in Microsoft Word, and so use straight lines.)
>
> As on flowcharts, data flow lines flow top to bottom and left to right unless noted via arrows.
>
> To distinguish them from flow-of-control lines as in a flowchart, we sometimes use double lines, as shown here.

This DFD shows that the input data is used in making the decision P as well as in the functions A and B. However, only A's or B's data is used in the final output. The true/false condition P has no output, as it is not a process or function, but is only a decision as to whether to use A or B.

If-Then-Else Verification Check

To check your work, ask yourself two questions:

- If P is true, then does doing A do F, all of F, and nothing but F; and
- If P is false, does doing B accomplish F, all of F, and nothing but F.

If so, your If-Then-Else structure is correct.

For an additional type of check, see also "Boundary Conditions", p.46 below.

Extended Example – ACL access

At this point, let's expand some of the If-Then-Else structures in our example program. (There'll be more later.)

Here's the resulting Nassi-Schneiderman chart of our example, so far:

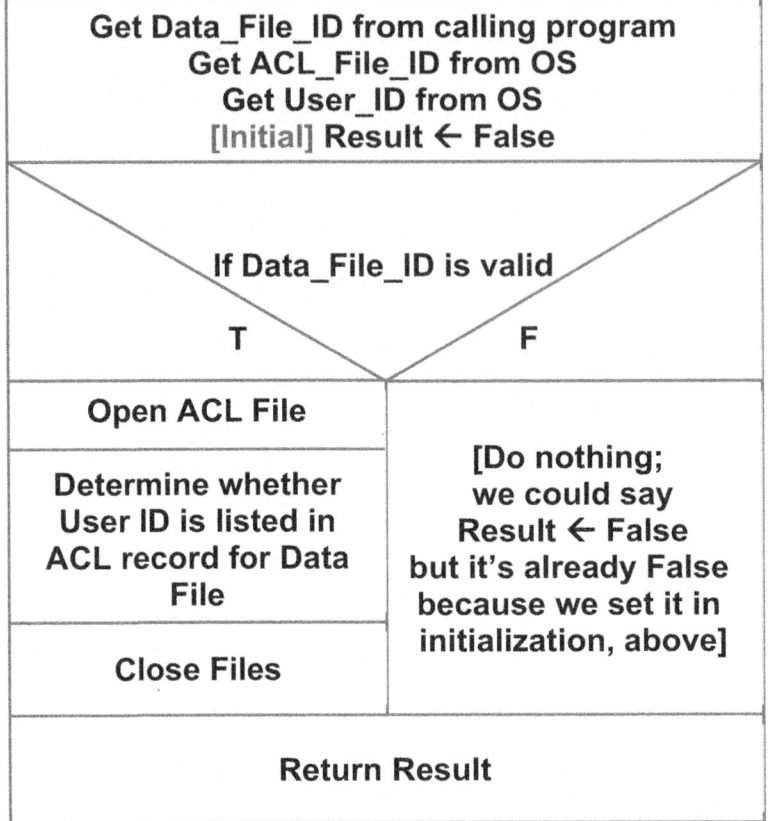

Note that this data pre-validation test and step is extremely common in programming. It's important to make sure the data is valid before we try to process it[31].

---

[31] This is similar to mathematics, in a way: Suppose we have a math equation $Y = 1 / X$. What if X happens to be zero? We can't divide by zero! So before we handle that equation, we'd better be sure that X is not zero. Similarly, we need to make sure our data is valid before we attempt to process it.

Do-While (Iteration)

> *"All of life is iterative. It goes back to the point I made earlier, which is you can't a priori know enough to even ask the right questions."*
> – Grady Booch [emphasis added]
>
> *"I gain weight and lose it again in inevitable cycles."*
> – Gerard Depardieu
>
> *"Until someone is prepared to lay out the systemic problem, we will simply go through cycles … ."*
> – Newt Gingrich

The `Do-While` (or simply `While`) structure forms loops. It repeats the execution of a process several times (usually with different parameters). Use `Do-While` when function F is performed by repeating some subfunction A zero or more times.

Let P be a true/false condition that will control the repetition of the subfunction A. P will tell us when A still needs to be continued and repeated again, or when A is complete and has accomplished F. At that point, the loop needs to be terminated. Then the overall function F is performed by performing A repetitively while P is true, and then stopping when P becomes false.

Note that A must not only perform a processing subfunction but *must* also eventually change P from true to false. If it does not, then an infinite and nonterminating loop will result. To avoid that, process A is almost always composed of substructures, one of which triggers that test P. It is generally a sequence of subfunctions and conditional structures.

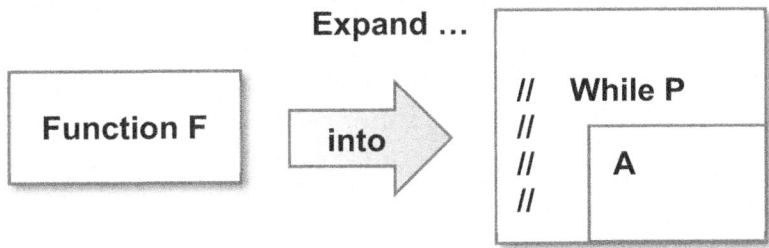

When to use the Do-While structure

Choose the `Do-While` structure when we need to do something <u>zero</u> or more times, over until it's done.

Do-While Example – Factorial

This time a mathematical example: One method[32] (or algorithm) for calculating the factorial function N! is to repetitively multiply 1 × 2 × 3 × 4 ... × N. We can express this mathematically as:

$$R = \prod_{i=1, N} i$$

Where the capital Pi (Π) means repetitive multiplication of terms, much as capital sigma (Σ) means repetitive addition of terms. Don't let the formula concern you, it's only here for the math buffs. We won't use it again. It's just a compact math jargon for saying we repetitively multiply until we get to N.

This could be expressed in pseudo-code as:

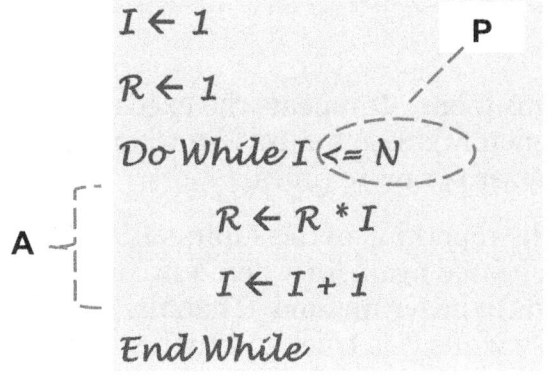

[The result R is N!]

Note:

The left-pointing arrow (←) means "assignment" of the value on the right to the variable on the left. The first line, "I ← 1", could be read as "assign 1 to I" or "I gets 1" or "set I to 1" or "I is set to 1" or "make I equal to 1" (though that last may be less than ideal). For more information see "Assignments and Variables" on p.36.

Most programming languages and notations use the equal sign "=" for this. A few use ":=".

As in math, the "<=" simply means "less than or equal to".

This is a small program in its own right. It's a **Sequence** within a **While** within a **Sequence**. Do you see why? The parts of the outer sequence are the initial assignment statements and the **While** structure. The inner sequence is the two assignments in **A**.

The condition **P** in the **While** is "I <= N", which is a true/false Boolean logic statement. In other words, at any given point in time, it will either be true or false that I is less than or equal to N. When I *is* less than or equal to N, the loop continues and the body **A** is executed again. When I *is not* less than or equal to N, the loop terminates (exits).

---

[32] Another method uses Recursion, but that is beyond our present scope.

Do-While (Iteration)

The body A of the `while` structure is the inner `Sequence` of two assignment statements (R ← R * I; I ← I + 1).[33]

Now, the looping structures (`while` and `Until`) do not necessarily have to involve counting as we have used them here. They could involve any looping condition. Another common use is for reading data, where we very commonly have a structure like:

> *Read Data Line*
> *While not EOF Do*
>   *Process data*
>   *Read Data Line*
> *End While*

> Note:
>
> "*EOF*" means "End of File". The structure reads and processes data from a file until it reaches the end of the file when there is no more data to read. Then it stops.

Note that our choices of different kinds of loop structures and EOF tests depend on our programming language and operating system. Some test for End of File *before* even trying to read. Some test for End of File *while* trying to read but encountering the file's end as they do it. Either is possible and valid and is largely out of the programmer's control. However, each possibility dictates that we use a different type of looping structure. We may need to use a `While` or an `Until` (see below). We may need to imbed the loop in an `If not EOF Then Do` structure. We may need two `Read Data Line` statements as above or only need the inner statement.

Do-While Pseudo-code

> *While P*
>
> *A*
>
> *End While*

> Note that different languages and different pseudo-code conventions often use variants of the `while` syntax. The following are all fairly common: "`while P`", "`Do while P`", and "`while P Do`". Similarly, some delimit the end with "`End`", "`End while`", "`Next`", "`End Do`", "`Od`" ("do" spelled backward), a semicolon, or have no ending delimiter at all. Some consider the `Do` to be part of the `while` syntax itself, and some consider it an imbedded block forming the `while`'s body. All are equivalent. In pseudo-

---

[33] For what it's worth, if we wanted to, there are also a couple of ways to write a routine that calculates N! for N >= 0 not just N >= 1, as here. That is because mathematically 0! = 1! = 1. But it isn't quite as simple as just staring I out at 0 instead of 1. (Try it yourself as an exercise.)

code, you can take your pick and use whatever makes most sense and is most comfortable to you. In an actual program, we must use whatever our programming language requires.

Do-While Flowchart

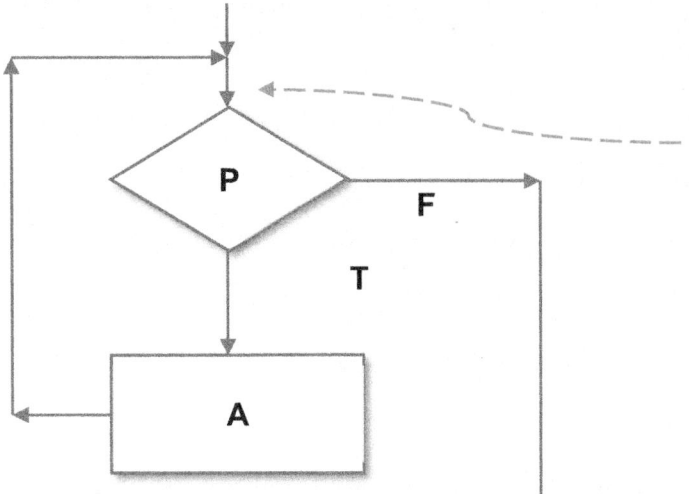

Note: Although it is beyond the scope of our discussion, more advanced students may note that this is where the "loop invariant" goes (if we're using one). It's right at the junction before the test for P. (More on this, later.)

Note: Remember that the boxes in flowcharts are not the smallest indivisible programming units. So boxes cannot be utilized by themselves and connected with flow lines any which way. (For example, no matter how complex A is, there's only one exit from the A box and that is back to the P conditional box. And there's only one exit from the `while` structure, and that's the false F exit from the P box.) The entire fundamental *structures*, not their component boxes, are "atomic" (i.e., indivisible primitives). This is one of the chief advantages of Nassi-Schneiderman charts over flowcharts: it does not tend to mislead in this regard.

Do-While Nassi-Schneiderman Chart

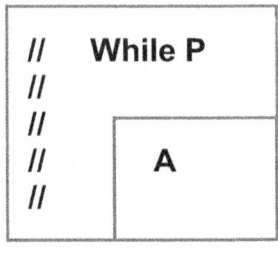

Or

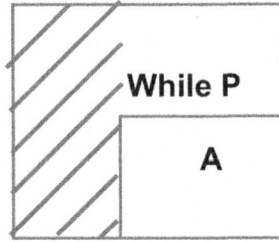

Since it's mentioned in passing above, note that N-S Charts have no built-in way to show loop invariants. We can show them as a comment in the `while` part of the box or perhaps in the A part of the box before the body A itself. Better, we might use an **Assert** statement (see below).

Strictly speaking, the more graphical representations with the hatching or with blanks are closer to the original design of N-S charts. But we will use the simpler first one with the slashes because it is both clear and easier to do in MS Word.

Do-While (Iteration)

Or

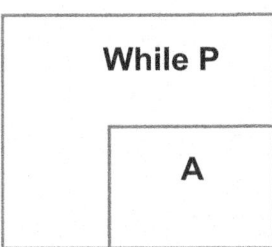

Use 1 to 3 slashes per line, or none (as here), as seems reasonable to you. All are valid.

Personally, I like the hatching or the slashes, as they seem to be clearer than a blank box.

Both the flowchart and N-S chart above show that while **P** is true, then **A** will be repeated; and when **P** becomes false, then the repetition stops.

Incidentally, what happens in the case where **P** just happens to be false the first time it is executed? Look at the charts. In this case, **A** is never executed at all! This is the major difference between the `While` structure and the `Repeat-Until` structure discussed below (p.53).

Do-While Data Flow Diagram

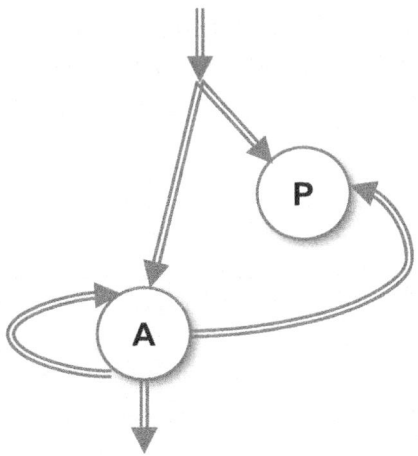

This DFD says that the input data is used in making the decision **P** as well as in the function **A**. Furthermore, data from **A** passes back to **P**. In other words, **A** modifies **P**. This is necessary for it to eventually change **P** from `True` to `False` so that the loop will terminate. We don't want an infinite loop that runs forever! Additionally, data from **A** loops back to itself (to **A**). That's what the structure is all about, really: repeating **A** multiple times with each iteration feeding back into the next. Finally, the (cumulative) data from **A** forms the final output data for the structure as a whole. As with the `If-Then-Else` structure, true/false conditionals like **P** do not change data or contribute to the output.

Do-While Verification Check

Since this structure is more complex, so are its verification questions. There are several:

- First, is termination guaranteed (as opposed to the possibility of an infinite loop)? Ask: Does repeatedly doing process A eventually make condition P false?
- Next, whenever P is false, then is doing F (and all of F) accomplished by doing nothing further? What this is really asking is, when we quit, do we have the right result and do we quit at the right time?
- In fact, if P is false at the beginning, then does doing nothing at all do F and all of F? A quick example: Consider factorial again. If we tried 1! (one factorial), then P would initially be `false`. In that case, is 1! equal to 1? Yes, it is, and that's the right mathematical answer. So, we've done (that part of) the loop right.
- Be sure to check the boundaries: Are they right? Does it work for them? Again, in factorial, make sure it works for I = N and I = 1 and even I = 0.
- Finally, whenever P is true, does doing process A followed by doing all of F (i.e., repeatedly looping again) accomplish F, all of F, and nothing but F?

This may seem tedious. (But really, we should actually add a bit *more* regarding "loop invariants". That's more advanced and is not required when we're beginning programmers[34]. So let's save that for "Appendix 4 – Loop Invariants", p.119 below.) Nevertheless, these verification questions are well worth the effort to achieve correctness and make sure our program is working as it should. And compared to other methodologies this isn't bad. Compared the more difficult and costly effort of maintenance, debugging, and diagnosing errors later, this is fairly simple. So it actually saves us a lot of time and effort.

Boundary Conditions

Another verification test alluded to above is to test the <u>boundary conditions</u> or <u>edge cases</u>, the situations at the minimum and maximum conditions in which the loop is expected to run. This applies to loops of any kind (`While`, `Until`, or `For`). For instance, if a loop is expected to process cases of zip codes of a certain city from 23456 to 23567, then check what happens if the zip code is 23455, 23456, 23567, and 23568. Codes 23455 and 23468 should be rejected, but 23456 and 23567 should be processed successfully, producing the correct results.

Notice that while boundary condition checks are particularly useful in loops, they also fit `If-Then-Else` structures and are useful there, as well.

---

[34] Because you asked (for advanced users only): "A <u>loop invariant</u> is a property of a program loop that is true before (and after) each iteration. It is a logical assertion, sometimes checked within the code by an assertion call. Knowing its invariant(s) is essential in understanding the effect of a loop. ... From a programming methodology viewpoint, the loop invariant can be viewed as a more abstract specification of the loop, which characterizes the deeper purpose of the loop beyond the details of this implementation" (Wikipedia). More on this in "Appendix 4 – Loop Invariants", below.

Do-While (Iteration)

Extended Example

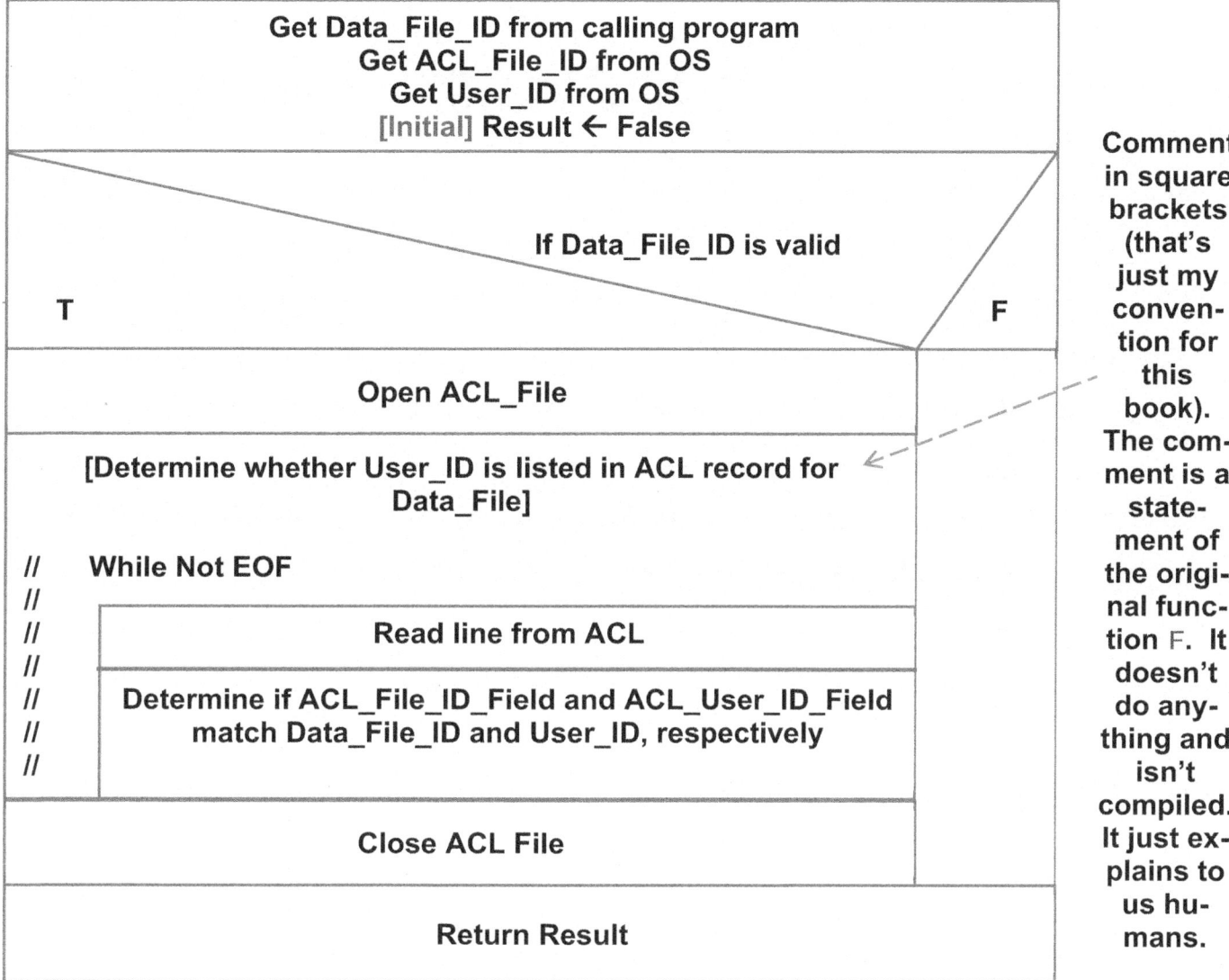

Next, let's break down and detail out that process within the while loop (Read line, determine match, etc.).

Here's the result of our example:

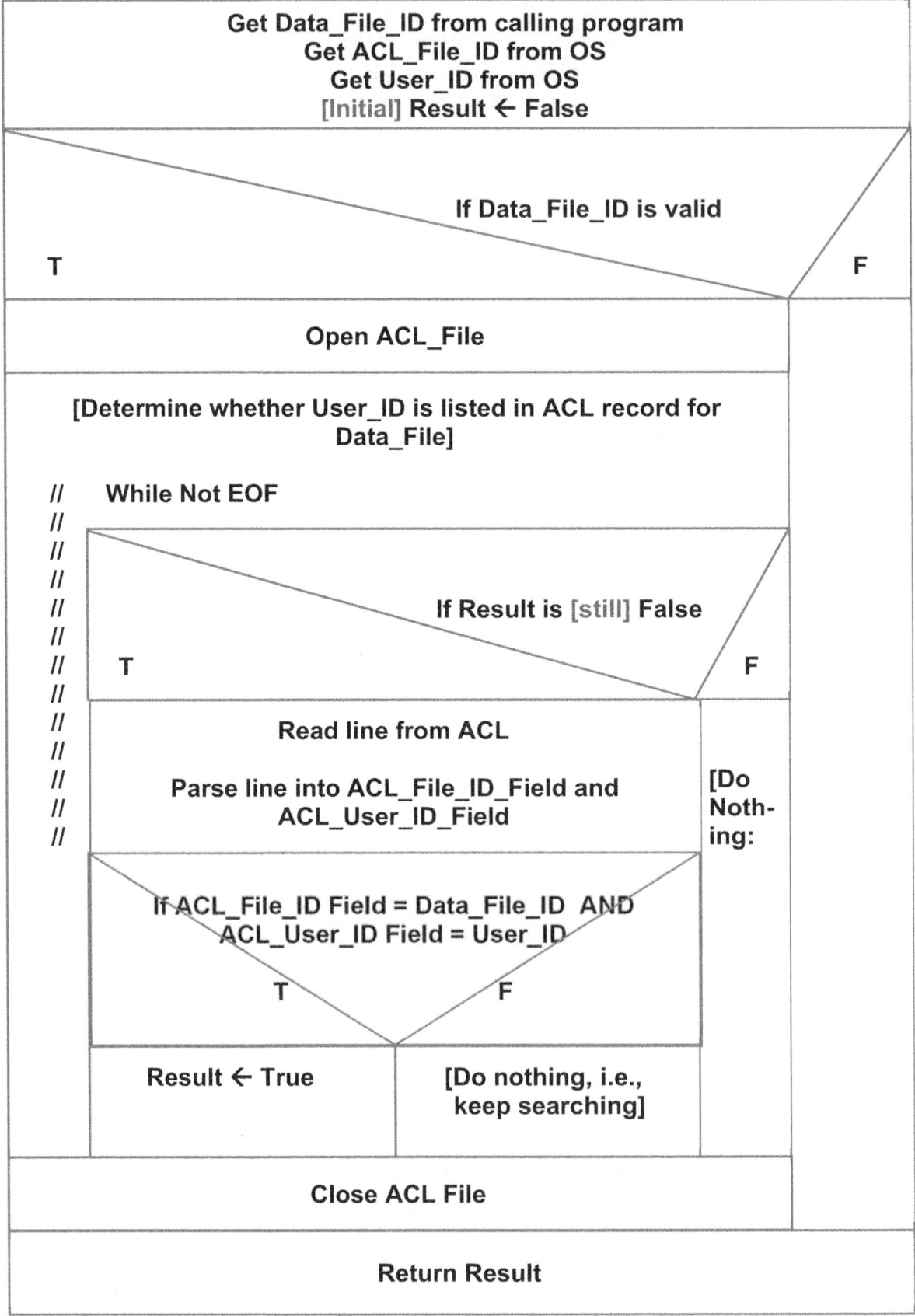

That's an oversimplification. That's not really the *final* program at all. How do we read a line from a file, e.g., from the ACL? For that matter, how do we open and close files? How do we parse the lines of the ACL into the `ACL_User_ID` and `ACL_File_ID` fields? How do we get the User ID from the operating system? How do we get the ACL from the OS? That's sensitive information. Is it encrypted? Is the encryption at the file level, the individual record or data line level, or both? How do we decrypt it? There's much yet to be determined and yet to be detailed in our program. But the above structure will suffice for our example. Aside from the level of detail, it is complete and accomplishes the problem statement that it is supposed to accomplish.

Nesting structures

We pretty much always have nested structures, one structure within another. In Nassi-Schneiderman notation, they can be diagrammed either of two equivalent ways:

The simpler and more conventional way:

```
// For X = 1 to N
    // For Y = 1 to M
        //
        Do something N × M times
```

Or the more contoured way which shows the nesting more clearly:

```
// For X = 1 to N
    // For Y = 1 to M
        //
        Do something N × M times
        //
```

As they're completely equivalent, use whichever way is clearer and more comfortable. I'll use the simpler way, which is more common and conventional. But do feel free to use the more contoured way if it helps you.

Remember that diagramming is useful but is only a tool, not an end in itself. We needn't use charts and diagrams unless they help. I find that N-S charts and pseudo-code generally do help, especially when I'm trying to work out complex logic. But if they don't, then skip them! However, when beginning programming I strongly urge you to always use them!

That gets to the point of why we use diagramming (of either sort) in the first place. It's a tool for use in the design and development stages of programming. It's not a method to document the code we've already written. Back in "ancient history", some employers used to require a flowchart to document all programs after they're done. This is useless, as it won't be kept up to date, and it's the programming language code, not the charts, that is the master document. The same is true of pseudo-code, though I've never heard of anyone requiring it. The only exceptions to either diagramming or pseudo-code are programming courses: if the instructor requires it as part of an assignment, then do it. But in "real life" it's a tool in our tool chest and like any tool, we make good use of it when it fits, but don't use it when it doesn't.

Valid Variants and Extended Control Structures

> *"God, grant me the serenity to accept the things I cannot change,*
> *The courage to change the things I can,*
> *And wisdom to know the difference."*
>
> — Reinhold Niebuhr, Theologian, 1944

Why variants?

The following structures are valid variants that can be derived from the three fundamental structures, above (pp. 21ff). Most other structures *not* described here are **not** valid and will only cause problems.

Perhaps we should stop here and leave well enough alone. But for completeness – and usefulness! – let's continue. Not including the valid alternates might invite people to use invalid pseudo-structures and cause themselves trouble.

These valid variants are formed by unraveling or adding to the `Do-While` and `Repeat-Until` loops. They are valid because they are formed from the "big three", above. That's also why the "Unsafe Structures" (p.79) are not valid: those are tangled and cannot be unraveled.

For instance, a loop that does function `A` for `n` iterations can be replaced by sequence of

- a loop that does `A` for `(n-1)` iterations,
- followed by one final function `A`.

Or, depending on the situation, it can be

- a sequence of `A`
- followed by a loop of `n-1` iterations.

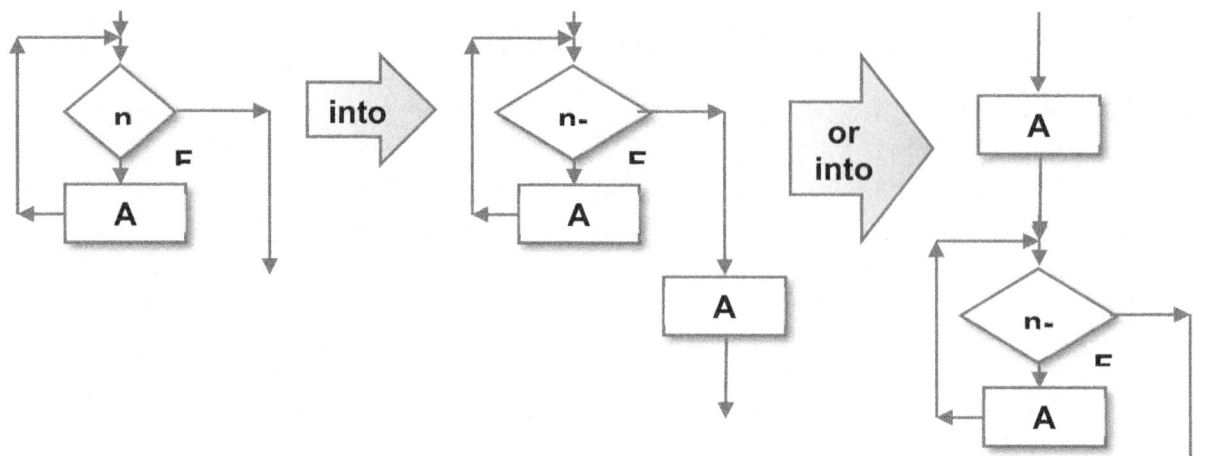

Either way, A is done n times. If carried out to the extreme we'd have a simple, though lengthy, **sequence** structure with n copies of A:

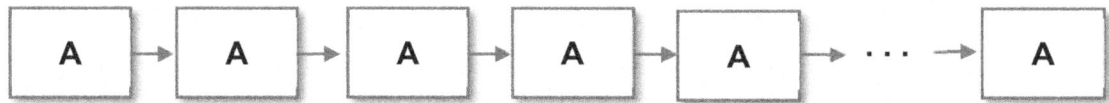

Here, then, are the *only* safe additional structures:

Repeat-Until

> *"Those who cannot remember the past are condemned to repeat it."*
> — George Santayana, 1905, <u>The Life of Reason...</u>
>
> *"Lather, Rinse, Repeat"*
> — *Instructions on a shampoo bottle*
>
> *"If something is worth saying, it is worth saying three times over."*
> — *Steven Magee*

Use the `Repeat-Until` (or simply `Until` or `Repeat`) structure when function `F` is performed by repeating some subfunction `A` one or more times. It is like `While` (so we'll will not repeat or belabor the similarities). However, with `Repeat-Until`, the loop is *always* executed *at least* once because the test is at the end, not the beginning.

`Repeat-Until` can be derived from `While` (as shown below; pp.56, 89, and 90). In fact, in context of an appropriate encompassing `Sequence`, either one can be used in most circumstances. This does ***not*** mean that they are equivalent or interchangeable without some tweaking. After all, one is always executed at least once, and the other isn't. `Repeat-Until` is more common in some programming languages. However, it is more troublesome, harder to verify correct, and more error-prone than `While`. `While` is generally preferred over `Until` for those reasons. Additionally, when seen in the proper context (which is important), I have found that `While` is more commonly *needed* in most real-life programming situations than is `Until`.

When to use the Repeat-Until structure

Choose the `Repeat-Until` structure when we need to do something <u>one</u> or more times, until it's done. Note that the `Do-While` structure repeats <u>zero</u> or more times and the `Repeat-Until` structure repeats <u>one</u> or more times. This is their main distinction.

Repeat-Until Example – Factorial

Let's look at how to do the same factorial function as in our When to use the Do-While structure

Choose the `Do-While` structure when we need to do something <u>zero</u> or more times, over until it's done.

Do-While Example, above (p.41):

```
I ← 1
R ← 1
Repeat
    ┌ ─ ─
A ─┤    R ← R * I
    │
    └   I ← I + 1          ─ ─ ─ P
Until (I > (N-1))
```

When I *is not* greater than (N-1) (i.e., when I is less than or equal to (N-1)), the loop continues and the body A is executed again. When I *is* greater than (N-1), the loop terminates (exits). So, the result, again R is N!, N factorial.

Note that the condition P in the Repeat-Until is "I > (N-1)", not "I > N". That's because by the time that I is tested at the end of the loop, the interim result R has already been multiplied by I. (Recall that in a Do-While, it is tested at the beginning and R has not yet been multiplied by I.) So Repeat-Until results in an additional execution of the loop body A. We adjust by testing against N-1 instead of against N. So although the overall result is the same, the Repeat-Until method of reaching it is a little trickier. This is one of the reasons that Do-While loops are often easier and better to use than Repeat-Until loops.

In many cases, we could also convert a Do-While into a Repeat-Until by adjusting the initial conditions rather than by adjusting the condition P. For instance, we could change I ← 1 and R ← 1 into I ← 0 and R ← 0. (However, that won't work in this case.) Again, this shows why Do-While loops are often (but not always) better.

Repeat-Until Pseudo-code

```
Repeat
    A
Until P
```

> As usual, there are various language conventions that might be used here. Some omit the **Repeat** keyword, some swap **Repeat** and **Until**, some use block delimiters like **Do** and **End**, some that eliminate **Repeat** move the **Until** to the beginning while others do not, and so forth. As always, all are equivalent, but because you'll see variants, it's worth mentioning them so you know the equivalences and know what you're seeing.

Repeat-Until

Repeat-Until Flowchart

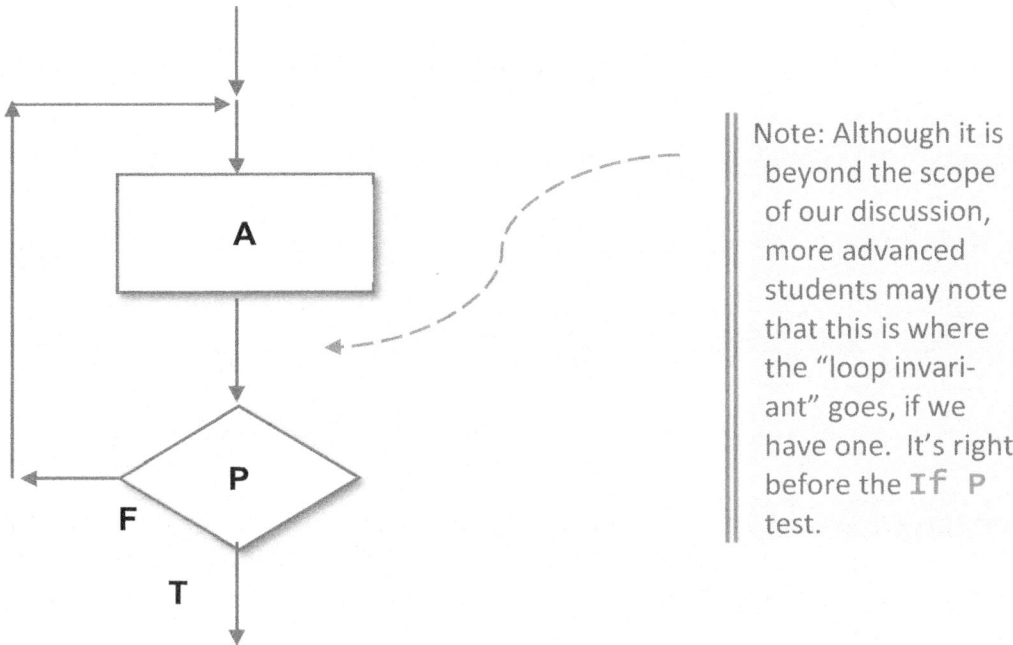

Note: Although it is beyond the scope of our discussion, more advanced students may note that this is where the "loop invariant" goes, if we have one. It's right before the If P test.

Unlike `While`, `Repeat-Until` is always executed *at least once*, even if P is initially False.

Repeat-Until Nassi-Schneiderman Chart

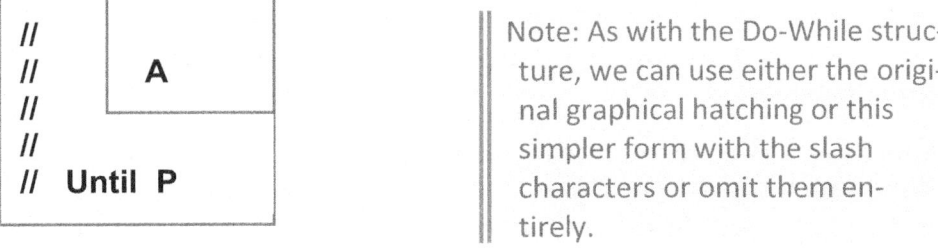

Note: As with the Do-While structure, we can use either the original graphical hatching or this simpler form with the slash characters or omit them entirely.

As usual, both the above flow- and N-S charts show that A will be repeated until P becomes true, then when P becomes false, the repetition stops.

Repeat-Until Data Flow Diagram

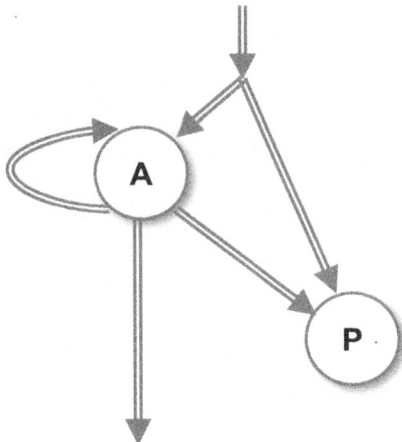

Note that this DFD is identical to the Do-While Data Flow Diagram (p.45). You may verify this by trying to describe this `Repeat-Until` DFD. You should find that the description of the `While` DFD still fits.

Repeat-Until Verification Check

Verifying the `Repeat-Until` structure is similar to verifying the `While` structure: Make sure it eventually terminates and is not an infinite loop, and make sure that doing A the right number of times does accomplish F.

However, this can get more complex and tedious than a simple `While`. That is one reason that formal mathematical program correctness verifiers prefer `While` to `Until`. (But since we're not doing mathematical proofs of correctness, we can use `Repeat-Until` when appropriate.)

Tedious though it is, the verification questions are only the combination of both of the two verifications for `Sequence` and `While`. So we will not repeat them here. In fact, it is easiest, to simply re-cast the structure as a `Sequence` and a `While`, and then to verify that.

Remember, the verifications are not an end in themselves. So don't get bogged down in them or wrapped round the axle. They're simply a useful tool as a cross-check, like checking your work in a math problem. Use them to make sure that the structures actually do what we want them to accomplish.

Repeat-Until vs Do-While

This subsection is optional for more advanced readers, so feel free to omit it and skip to "

Select Case", p.59 below.

Although while and Until loops are not directly interchangeable without modification, we can convert one to another with a little additional work. The main purpose of this is to show that the fundamental three structures are sufficient. That is, if we were concerned that Repeat-Until is not *really* one of the "big three", we can convert it into a structure using only the fundamental three. Or if we think we need a Repeat-Until loop, we can with a little extra work use a while instead. So, we are free to use either structure that works. (And of course, the reverse conversion works, also: we can similarly convert whiles into Repeat-Untils.)

For advanced readers who are interested, the *process* of conversion is shown in "Appendix 1 – Conversion of Repeat-Until to and from Do-while". The *result* is as follows:

This Repeat-Until:

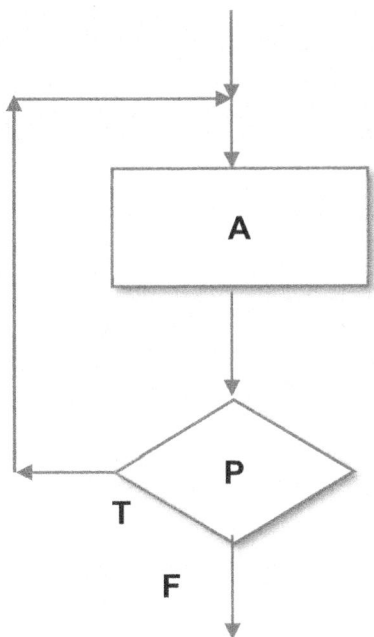

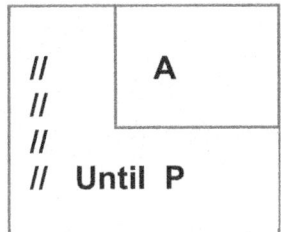

Can be converted into this `Do-While`:

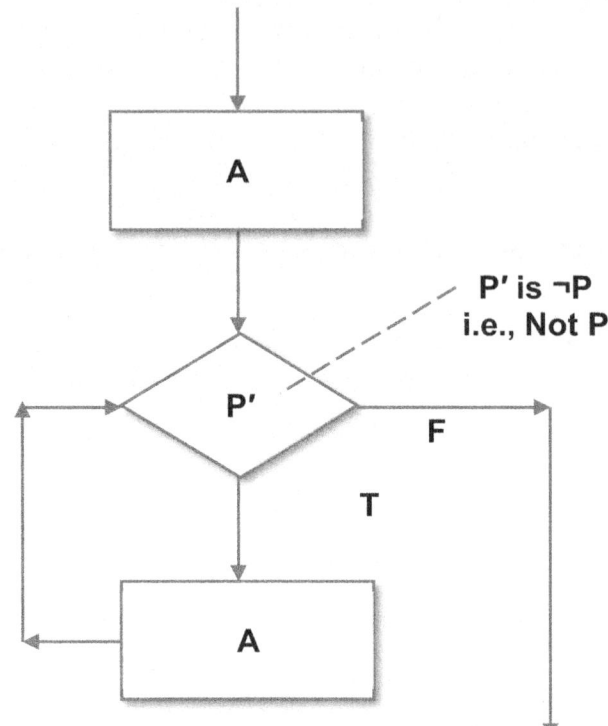

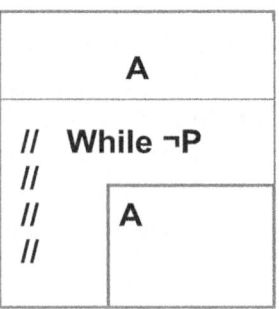

Conversion of `While` into `If-Then` and `Repeat-Until`

Finally, we can see by similar reasoning that a `While` is equivalent to an `Until` embedded in an `If-Then`. Let's relegate this to the appendix. Suffice it to say here that, "`While P Do A`" is equivalent to "`If P Then Repeat A Until Not P`".

There is, perhaps, less use for turning a `While` into an `Until` like this, but nevertheless it can be done if necessary. I personally have found both equivalents most useful in day-to-day programming. They particularly seem to come in useful in real production systems when constructing loops that read and process data. They may be less useful in other contexts like object-oriented programs where (among other things) acquiring data is done differently by classes and objects themselves.

For details of the conversion processes, see "Appendix 1 – Conversion of **Repeat-Until** to and from **Do-While**" (p. 89).

Select Case

> *"We are all special cases."*
>
> – Albert Camus
>
> *"The shoe that fits one person pinches another; there is no recipe for living that suits all cases."*
>
> – Carl Jung
>
> *"Never go out to meet trouble. If you just sit still, nine <u>cases</u> out of ten, someone will intercept it before it reaches you."*
>
> – Calvin Coolidge
> [emphasis added]

Another valid extension is the `Case` or `Selection` structure[35]. This is really nothing more than multiple `If-Then-Else`s chained or nested together. So of course, it is a valid control structure.

When to use the Select Case structure

Choose the `Select Case` structure when we need to decide upon a choice between many alternatives. The basic `If-Then-Else` structure selects between only <u>two</u> alternatives. The extended `If-Then-ElseIf-Else` structure selects between several alternatives. When we find ourselves nesting several `If-Then-Else` structures deeply within each other or using many `ElseIf` clauses, it's often better and clearer to use a `Select Case` structure.

---

[35] In some languages it is called, called `Switch` or `Match`. In most languages, however, Match and Switch mean other things very different from this.

Select Case Pseudo-code

```
Select Case N
    When N1
        A
    When N2
        B
    When N3
        C
        :
        :
    Otherwise
        D
End Case
```

Note:

There are several ways that `Select Case` is used. In general, **N** is a variable or expression that represents half of an equality test that would appear in an `If` statement or structure. **N1, N2, N3**, etc. are the other halves of the test. So the tests would mean `If N = N1 then ... ElseIf N = N2 then ...` and so forth. `Case` lets us avoid writing all that out.

Sometimes the relational operator (greater, less than, equal, etc.) of the `If` test is required, but if omitted, then "`=`" is assumed.

This should be clearer below.

As always, notation varies. Some pseudo-code notations and some programming languages omit the keyword `Case`, some omit `Select`; some use the keyword `Case` instead of `When`; some replace `Otherwise` with `Case Else`; some use `End Select` instead of `End Case`; and so forth. Sometimes the initial expression **N** is omitted and only the conditions **N1, N2, N3**, etc., are used in the `When` (or `Case`) clauses. Sometimes a colon is required after the `When` clauses (i.e., after **N1, N2, N3**, etc.). Sometimes `Begin/End` or `Do/End` substructures abound. They're all just different ways of expressing the same thing.

Regardless of syntax of the individual programming language, `Select-Case` simply does this: Depending on some value test or series of tests, the *first matching* clause is executed and that's all. Then execution skips to the end of the structure. There can be as many `Cases` (`When` clauses) as are necessary. If none match, then the `Case-Else` or `Otherwise` clause is executed, if one exists. While `Case-Else`/`Otherwise` is optional, it should always be used because we can trap errors that way.

Select Case Example – net pay

```
Select Case (Gross Pay - Taxes)
    When > 1,000,000,000
        Print "You're a billionaire! Congratulations!"
    When > 1,000,000
        Print "You're a multimillionaire!"
    When = 1,000,000
        Print "You're (exactly) a millionaire!"
    When > 100,000
        Print "Six figures. Nice!"
        :
        :
    When <= 15,000
        Print "What can we do to help?"
    Otherwise
        Print "Error"
End Case
```

Note: Programming languages rarely allow the comma in numbers like 1,000,000 when they're constants. But in pseudo-code we can do pretty much whatever we want to do to make things clear. So I've included the commas.

The flowchart should clarify how `Select Case` works:

Select Case Flowchart

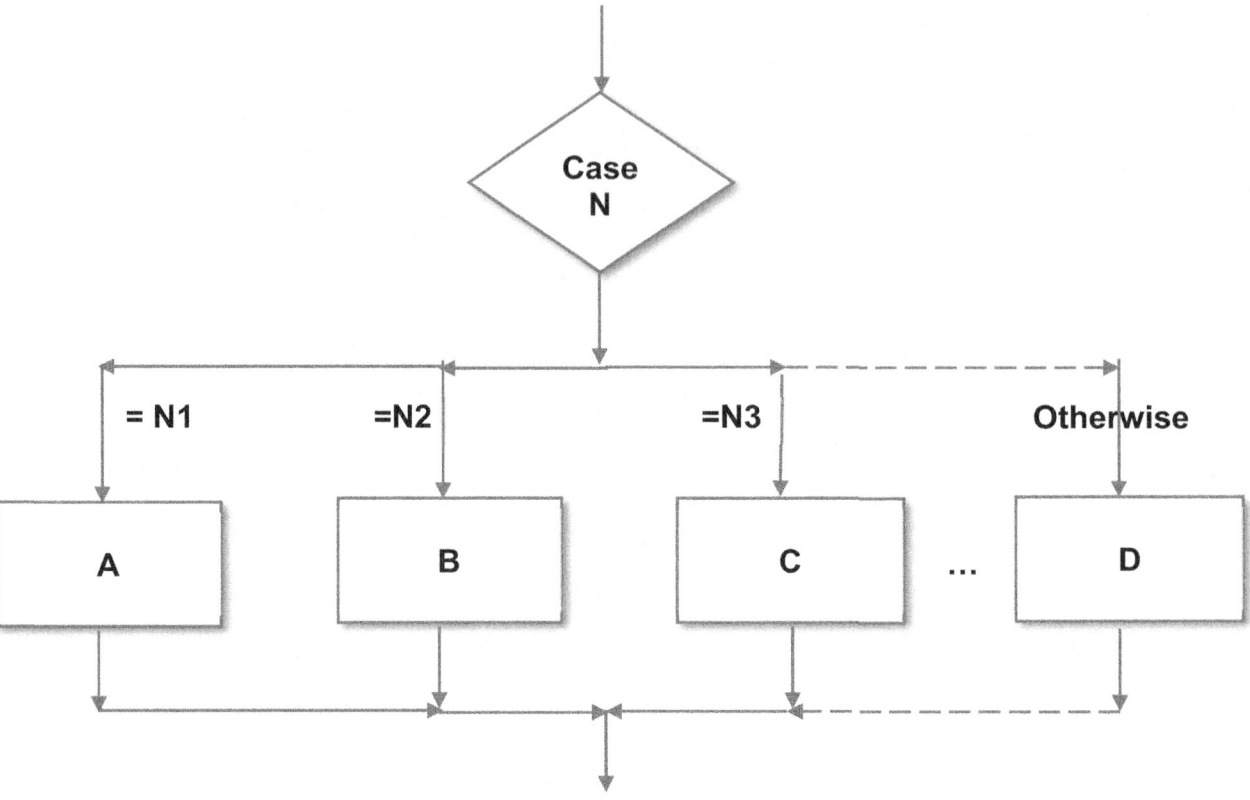

This is equivalent to the nested If-Then-ElseIf-Else structure shown under "Equivalence of Case to nested If-Then-Else", p.63 below.

As with all structures, it is most important to connect the outbound flowlines at the bottom – that's part of what makes this a structure rather than spaghetti code.

Select Case Nassi-Schneiderman Chart

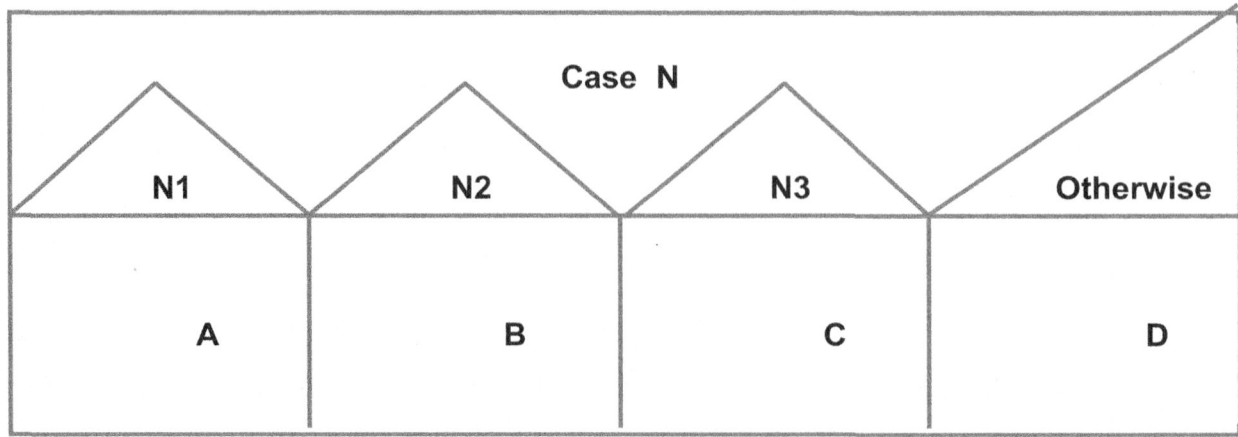

Or:

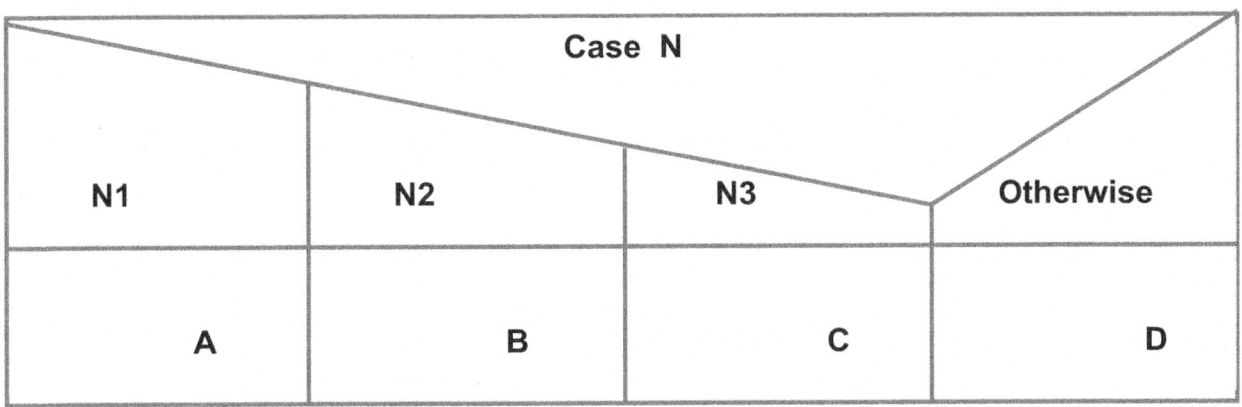

All three of the above charts mean that we select the first case in which N1, N2, N3, etc., matches N and we execute its corresponding procedure part A, B, C, etc., respectively.

And, to repeat, we can extend this for as many cases as we need.

Equivalence of Case to nested If-Then-Else

Just to illustrate the equivalence, here are the charts of the multiple, nested If-Then-Else structure that are equivalent to the Select-Case structure chart shown above. (This also illustrates the greater simplicity of using Case than If-Then-Else.)

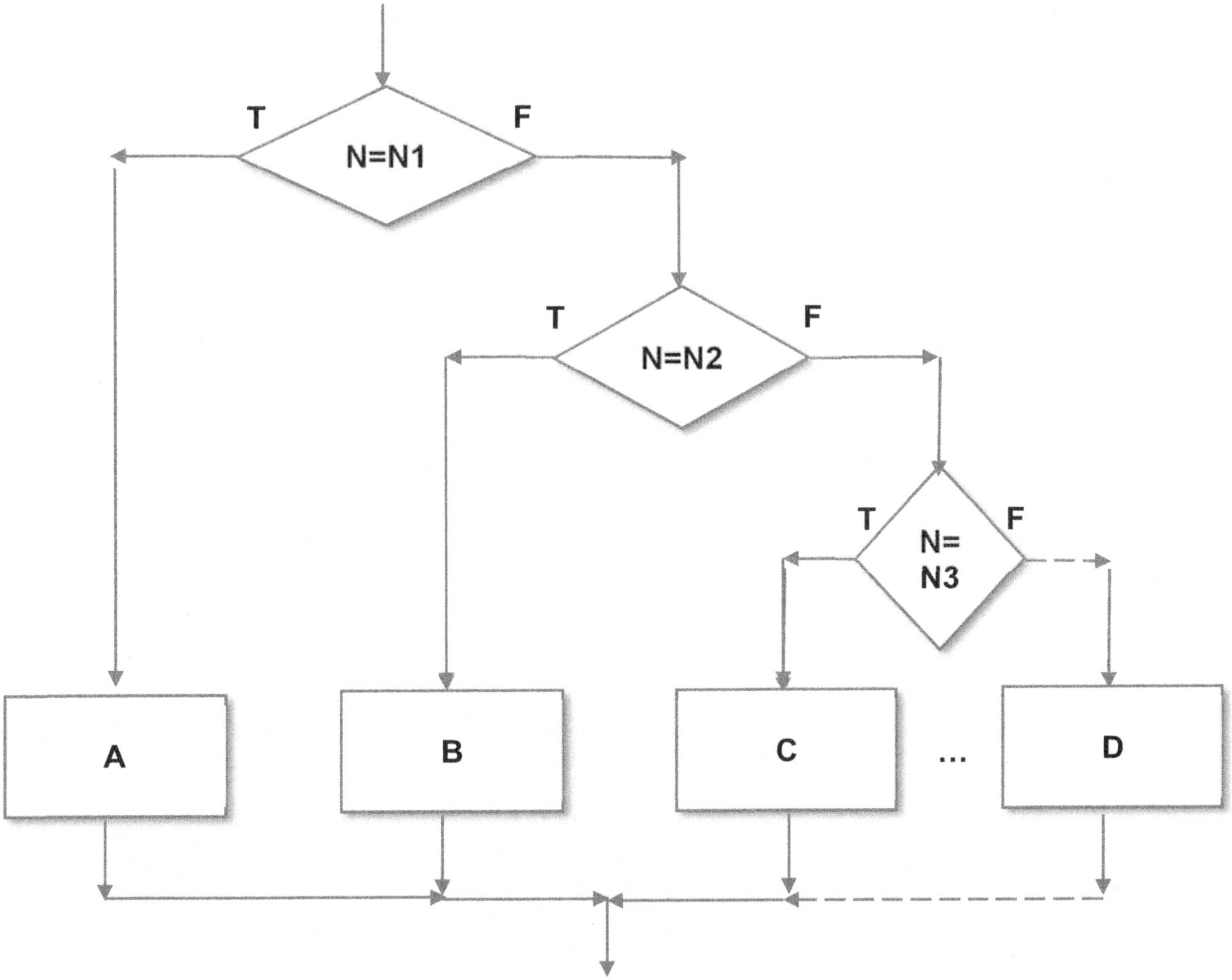

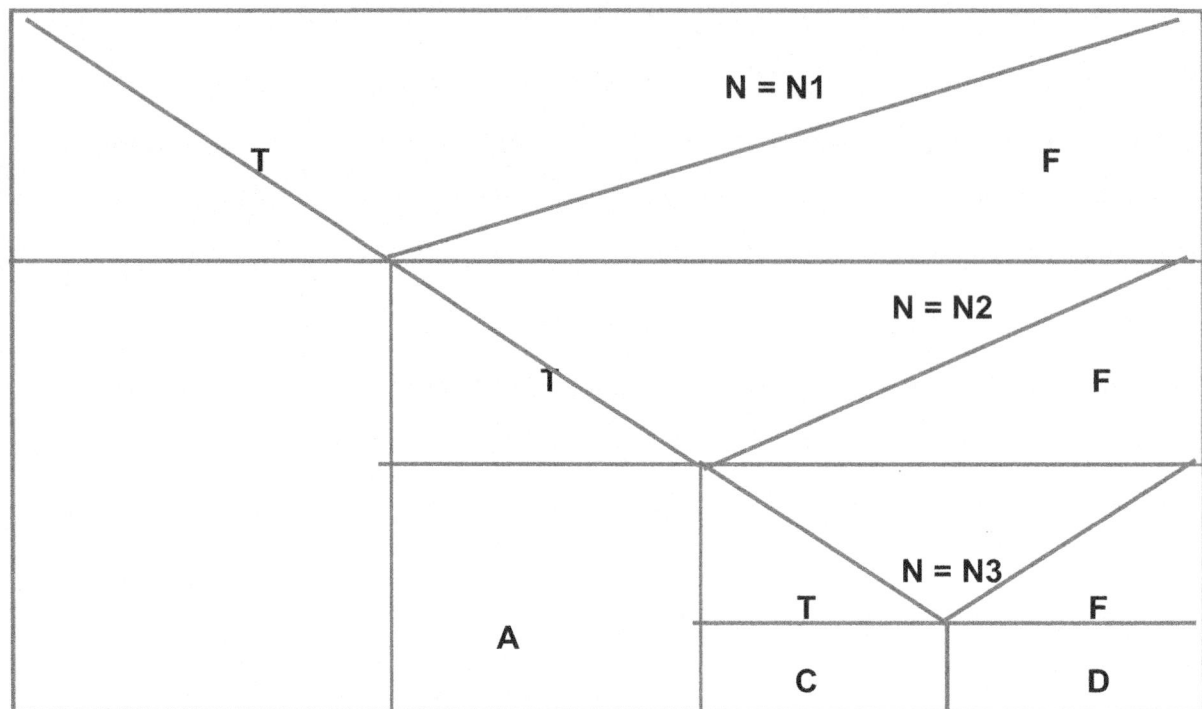

Select Case Data Flow Diagram

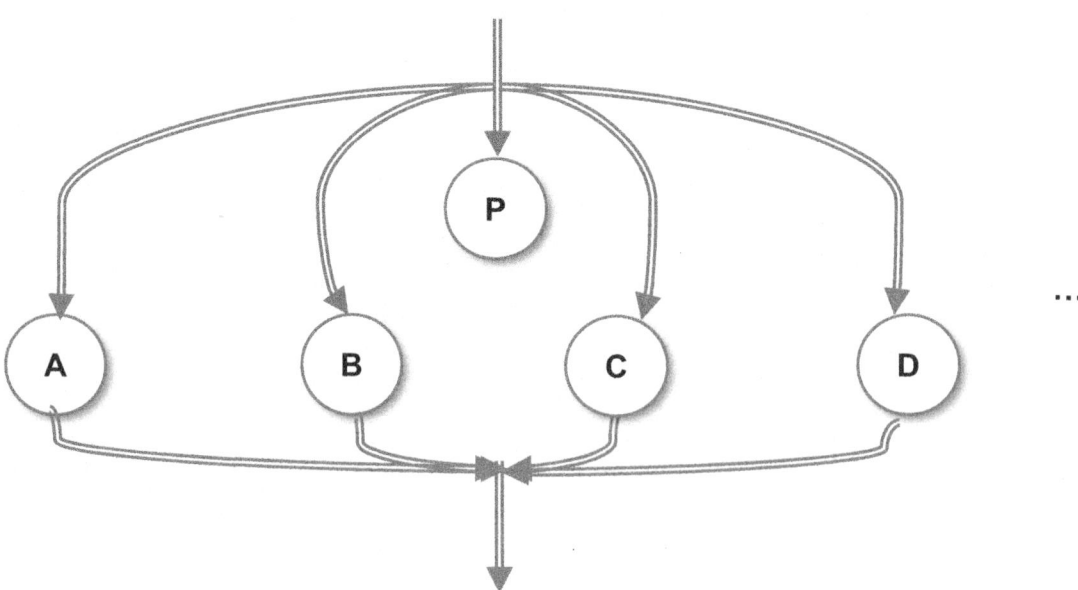

This DFD shows that the input data is used in making the decision P as well as in the functions A, B, C, and D. However, only A's, B's, C's, or D's data is used in the final output. The true/false condition P has no output, as it is not a process or function, but is only a decision as to whether to use A, B, C, or D.

More specifically, only the procedure executed is the one corresponding to whichever condition first is true. Let's say that the first true case is the third, N = 3. This would be procedure C. The other procedures (A, B, D, etc.) don't contribute to the output if they are never selected or executed. (

Select Case Verification Check

As with any of the derived extensions, to verify a Select-Case structure, convert it into its corresponding fundamental structure then verify that instead. In this case, convert a Case structure into a nested set of If-Then-Else structures, and ask the If-Then-Else verification questions of that structure:

- If P is true, then does doing A do F, all of F, and nothing but F; and
- If P is false, does doing B accomplish F, all of F, and nothing but F.

On Programming

For-Loop (Counted loop)

> "Not everything that can be counted counts, and not everything that counts can be counted."
>
> — William Bruce Cameron
> (often attributed to Albert Einstein)
>
> "Stop counting pages... you will never finish the book."
>
> — Deyth Banger

The last valid, derived extension we will deal with is the **For-Loop**. (For historical reasons[36] this is sometimes confusingly also called the **Do-Loop**. We will not do so here. Other language syntaxes call it **Do-For** or simply **For**. All are equivalent.)

This loop is a built-in statement with its own syntax in most programming languages. Its purpose is just to simplify and "package" a commonly needed set of functions. It is actually a built-in structure of structures "hidden" in a simplified syntax..

The simpler looping structures above (**While** and **Until**) do not necessarily have to involve *counting* per se. (Though our examples did.) However, such iterated, counted looping is the extremely common situation that the **For-Loop** was created to handle.

When to use the counted For-Loop structure

Choose the counted **For-Loop** structure when we need to do something a given number of times known in advance (or when a variable contains that number of times). The **Do-While** and **Repeat-Until** structures make their loop-or-quit decisions based on an arbitrary criterion. It could use any appropriate true-false test. However, the counted **For-Loop** repeats a given number of times based on the count.

For-Loop Example – Factorial

Let's take our factorial example again, this time with a **For-Loop**. (Review it first, if you wish, in the section on the "Do-While Example – Factorial" on p.42, above.) Here it is using a counted **For** loop:

---

[36] And "historical reasons", stripped of their historical context by passage of time, often become *hysterical* reasons.

```
R ← 1
For I = 1 to N by 1
    R ← R * I
End For
```

Note that this does the same thing as before but is much simpler to write. Similarly, if we wanted to add up all the odd numbers from 1 to N, we could write:

```
Sum ← 0
For I = 1 to N by 2
    Sum ← Sum + I
End For
```

And if we wanted to do something, call it function X, for M times, we could write:

```
For I = 1 to M
    X
End For
```

For-Loop Pseudo-code.

```
For V = S to E by C
    A
End For
```

Where V is a variable name, S is the starting value, E is the ending value that terminates the loop, and C is the increment. (If the increment is omitted, it is always assumed to be +1. Thus simply `For V = S to E`.)

But you've already guessed: notations vary. In some notations and programming languages the loop ends with `End`, in some with `End For`, in some with `Next`, in some `Loop`, and so forth. In some, the `For`-line itself ends with `Do` after the E- or C-clause. In some, every clause ends with a semicolon. And so it goes.

Note that we're approaching the rigorous syntax of a programming language now. This is doubly true since there is no simple N-S Chart symbology for a `For` loop – we draw it out by showing its component structures using the fundamental structures.

How a For Loop works

The structure will start with V = S and will execute process A then will increment V by C (add C to V, giving a new, updated value for V). Then it will loop again. When V is greater than or equal to E, the loop will stop.

For-Loop (Counted loop)

For-Loop Flowchart

This `For-Loop` is built using a `Do-While` structure, with the test before the body A:

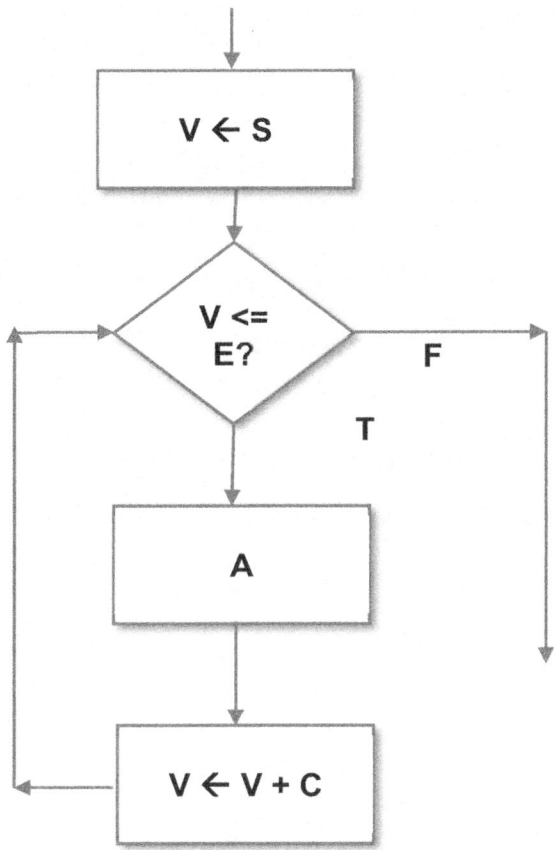

For loops can also be built using `Repeat-Until` structures with the test after the body A. Our example above uses `While` structures with the test before the body. The built-in `For` loop structures of many programming languages use `Until`s instead of `While`s. We won't show the `Until`-based `For` loops unless noted (except for their N-S chart, below). Rather, we stick with `While`-based `For`s only.

For-Loop Nassi-Schneiderman Chart

While-based *For-Loop*

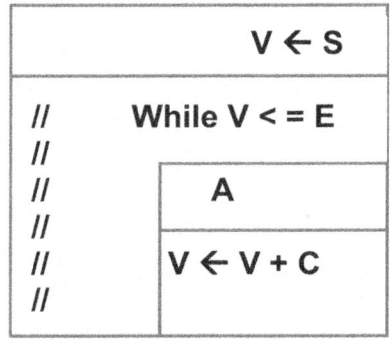

On Programming

The above `While`-based `For-Loop` chart shows that we start our count V at S. We continue looping and both executing A and counting, *while* V remains less than or equal to E. We increment our count (V) by C each time through the loop. We finally quit and exit the loop when V becomes greater than E, which it is guaranteed to eventually do.

*Until-based **For-Loop***

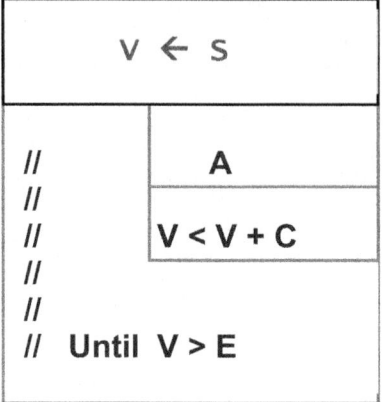

The operation of the `Until`-based `For-Loop` is like the `While`-based loop, above. Its interpretation is left to the reader (please try it!).

Please note that the condition P is different in each version. In the `While` form of the loop, it checks whether V <= E yet, and in the `Until` form, it checks whether V > E still. Why is this? What would happen if they were < and > (or <= and >=)? Would the loop body A be executed the same number of times in both `While` and `Until` forms then? Even with the different conditions (<= and >), do the two forms of look execute A exactly the same number of times? Why or why not? Think it through.

For-Loop (Counted loop)

For-Loop Data Flow Diagram

"Do-While" version of For-Loop DFD, showing data passed:

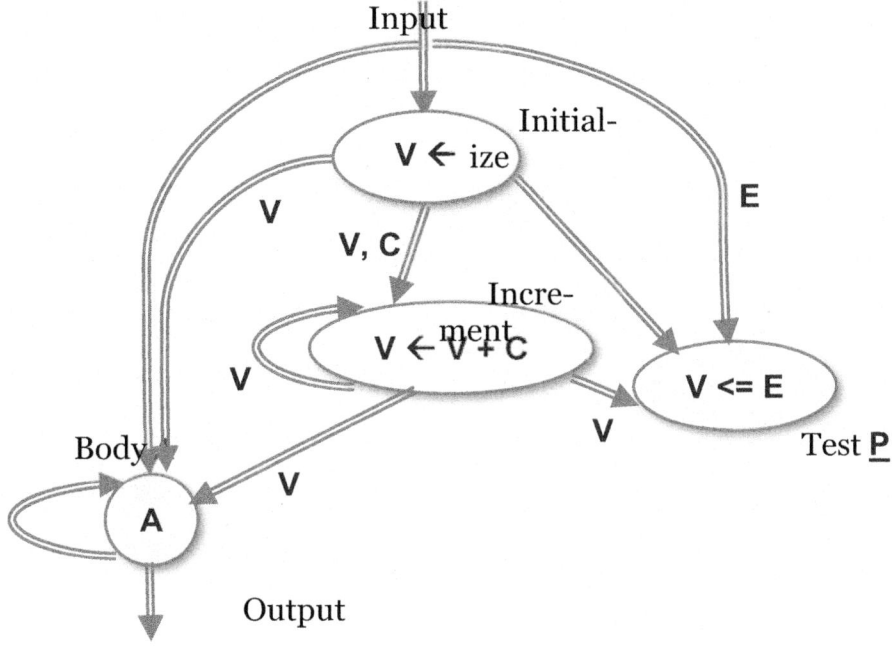

This DFD looks pretty complex. It says that the input data is used in

- initializing the counter V,
- in making the decision P (i.e., is V <= E?), and
- and in the loop body A.

Resulting data from A, after processing, is the output of the structure and function. The counter V may or may not directly play a part in the result, in A. The counter V itself eventually changes P from True to False by counting to E so that the loop will terminate.

The DFD for a counted For-Loop structure is more complex than the DFD for either a Do-While loop or a Repeat-Until loop structure. That's because it does more. However, it has more advantages: The For-Loop's flowcharts, N-S diagrams, code, verification are simpler and better. Perhaps most importantly, it *always* terminates.

It is impossible to have an infinite loop in a counted For-Loop structure. The loop always terminates because the count eventually hits the end and the loop exits. (In our example, V eventually counts up to become greater than E, which ends the loop.)

For-Loop Verification Check

In important respects this is actually easier to verify than an ordinary loop, since termination is *guaranteed*. (This requires that either C is positive and E is greater than S, or that C is negative and E is smaller than S.) In other respects, it's a little harder to verify since it's a slightly more complex structure, after all. As with all derived structures, we verify it only by verifying the parts. Try it yourself as an exercise.

On Programming

Another reason `For` loops are easier to use and check is that their "Boundary Conditions" (see p.46) are easier to check. Their boundary conditions are still very important, however. For instance, a common error is to either start or end the loop one off from where it should be. For example, counting from 1 to 10 when we should be counting from 0 to 9 or something like that.

For-Each (Object selection loop)

Many object-oriented languages (see "Object-oriented programming", p.7 above, and elsewhere throughout) also have a `For-Each` loop structure. It iteratively loops through each instance of a given object. The charts of the structure are essentially the same as the charts of the `Do-While`, `For-Loop`, and other loop structures. However, instead of the control variable (`I`, in our `For-Loop` examples) being a counted integer, it is an instance of the given object.

An example in pseudo-code that processes spreadsheet cells in a previously defined cell `Range` would look like this:

> *For Each aCell In Range*
>
>   *Call Process_Cell(aCell)*   [See footnote: 37]
>
> *End For*

This is an advanced structure primarily for object-oriented programming (and beyond our scope). However, it is mentioned in passing to illustrate the power of structured loops,]. Indeed `For-Each` is a very powerful and useful structure.

We would choose this structure when we need to process all elements or instances of an object.

---

[37] The subroutine `Call` statement is briefly discussed below (see "Subroutine", p83).

On Programming

Recursion

As noted above (p.15), _recursion_ is another form of repetition. In recursion, a program, usually a Subroutine (see below), calls or invokes itself to do part of the work. Recursion is resource-intensive and its internal implementation is specialized and unique. So not all languages allow recursion. Even when they do, its resource-intensive nature means it should be used carefully and perhaps infrequently. It is also not a structured programming concept and so is beyond our scope.

Recursion Example – Factorial

Let's take our factorial example again, this time with recusion. (Review it first, if you wish, in the section on the "Do-While Example – Factorial" on p.42, above.) Here it is using recursion. Instead of iterating or looping to calculate 1 × 2 × 3 × 4 × ... up to N, our Factorial function could call itself as follows:

> Factorial(N) ::=[38]
>
>   If N <= 1 then Factorial ← 1
>
>   Else Factorial ← N * Factorial(N-1)

(Note that this is merely an illustration to show what recursion is, not a recommendation. In fact, recursion is really not a very good way to calculate Factorial.)

---

[38] Recall that ::= means "is defined as".

On Programming

One more construct

> *"No complex adaptive system will succeed in adapting in a reasonable amount of time unless the adaptation can proceed subsystem by subsystem, each subsystem relatively independent of the others."*
> — *Christopher Alexander, Notes on the Synthesis of Form, 1964*

Subroutine

Another useful construct is the subroutine (or procedure, function, or subprogram[39]). Subroutines are like subcontracting out the details of a subordinate portion of our program. They're black boxes (p.13): At this point, we know *what* they do, but not *how*.

As we've done so far, we *could* include the entire program and all its details into our main program. However, it is often more convenient to do it separately as a subroutine. Our main program then calls the subroutine to perform a function, which leaves our main program simpler and clearer.

When we do something several times in different places (often with different input data), it's a good idea to use subroutines. Then we will code that part of the program once as a subroutine and simply call it in our main program. That avoids making our main program more complex by including it several times in different places. In addition, the system (operating system, utilities, etc.) will sometimes provide the routines to do various built-in functions. In that case, all we need to do is call them. What's more, they're usually much more efficient than anything we'd develop on our own, anyway.

So that's when we'd use a subroutine – when we want to subcontract-out some of our program because we don't want to use copies of the or similar same code in multiple places in our program. Sometimes, we also use a subroutine simply for clarity.

The charting symbol for calling or invoking a subroutine (whether in a flowchart or a Nassi-Schneiderman chart) is:

| CALL [name of subroutine or function] | or simply | [name of subroutine or function] |

---

[39] There are differences and nuances between these. For instance, a *function* routine can return a value for direct use, say in a formula. Subroutines can't do that, though they can manipulate data and change variable values. For our purposes, we'll loosely consider them all as essentially synonymous and just use "subroutine" as a generic term. (Strictly speaking, the term "subprocedure" would probably be more encompassing and accurate. However, its also more cumbersome).

with or without the "`Call`" command.

If that looks like a box within a box and seems confusing, we could put slashes or hash marks or something in the side parts of the box to more easily distinguish it.

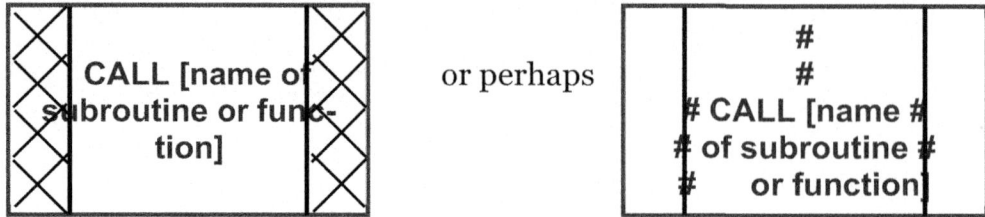

We put it this our chart when we subcontract the function or operation to a subprogram. Then later, we design the details of that function as a separate, named, program (unless it's a built-in system function). As noted above (p.11), this is part of the top-down process that relies on confidence, trust, even faith: What we define at a higher level, we will be able to flesh-out and detail in later steps in the lower levels yet to be coded[40].

Remember to ensure that each subroutine has only a single purpose or responsibility and doesn't include the kitchen sink. (This is especially critical for "Function" subprograms.) If we need more done, we use additional subroutines rather than lumping it all into one subroutine. Using our top-down stepwise refinement process should help in this regard.

Subroutines and functions are powerful. They are usually language-specific (i.e., each programming language implements them differently and with different syntax). And their usage can be either simple or quite complex. So, this is a mere introduction to the concept of subroutines. The details are beyond the scope of our discussion.

Incidentally, the calling program, not the subroutine, is responsible for checking any preconditions. For instance, calling `SquareRoot(-1)` will fail because the square root of a negative number is mathematically undefined[41]. So, the calling program needs to insure that `SquareRoot` is never called with a negative number as an argument. It needs to take "evasive action" by calling an error-handling routine to prevent such an occurrence *before* attempting the call.

---

[40] In a sense, even standalone main programs are subroutines, too. They are called or invoked by the user or by the operating system rather than by another program. Some languages explicitly term main programs a `Subroutine` with the title "`Main`". Others use the program or file name. Still others make a distinction between programs and subroutines. As always, different languages do it differently.

[41] At least in real numbers.

Unsafe Structures

> *"Danger, Will Robinson!"*
> -- <u>Lost in Space</u>, 1960s TV series

This is easy: ***Avoid all other structures*** than what we've presented so far*!*

There are various other structures, pseudo-structures, and programming language constructs that we encounter on occasion. Some have valid-sounding names, some have built-in programming language implementations, and some mere impostors of cleverly disguised spaghetti code. Most (dare we say *all*?) of these other structures are not valid and should not be used at all. Many are too problematic, too error prone, and too difficult to use and verify, to be worth attempting. This includes *all multiple-exit* or *test-in-the-middle* loops. Some invalid structures can even be found in structured programming textbooks. Avoid them all, as they only trick us into thinking that all's well when in fact it isn't.

Built-in programming language statements to avoid

Some structures are almost the opposite. This includes things like such as the various `Iterate`, `Leave`, `Exit-Loop`, `Go-To`[42], and `Break`, statements common in many programming languages. They are regularly decried as being "unstructured". However, *when their underlying charts are drawn and structured properly*, they can be found to be equivalent to a rather complex, but valid, structure. They exist for experts. So, *avoid them*, especially at first, because the surface simplicity hides the underlying complexity and its inherent problems. Avoid them also because the work we need to do to restructure them into valid structures is also complex and therefore problematic. It's far easier to never use them than it is to fix them when they cause problems.

Bottom line: They are simply not worth the trouble they cause. The exception is when used by experienced professionals who know exactly what they're doing and why they're using them – and who know the price they're paying when they do so.

There are also, of course, many other built-in programming language statements to *always* avoid (such as `Alter`[43]).

---

[42] In the rare case that a programming language does not have built-in block structures, the structures can be built "by hand" using `Go-To` statements. Other than that, `Go-To`s should always be avoided. Fortunately, most modern programming languages do include the legitimate block structures. So `Go-To` is not needed.

[43] `Alter`, in some languages, changes program code to do something other than what it says it does. Avoid it at all costs! It's a great example of the axiom that just because we <u>can</u> do something doesn't mean that we *should* do it or that it's a good idea!

On Programming

> Conversely, there are many other very useful built-in features to make good use of. The best guidance is to not use any but the legitimate structures discussed above until you know *what* these other structures do, *how* they do it, and what *you're* doing. Only then when you're sufficiently expert, should you make appropriate use of valid and useful features. Until then, use great caution!

Avoid these pseudo-"structures"!

There is no safe and valid way to directly exit from the middle of a loop or to have multiple exits from a loop. Period. Amen. Full stop.

Put another way, as seen above, all valid structures have exactly one entry point and one exit point. This might best be seen by contrasting with examples of invalid, unsafe structures below.

Sadly, these invalid structures are used all the time! In fact, *there is no correct and valid way to have multiple exits from a loop.* The single exit must be the one `P` test at either the beginning (`Do-While`) or end (`Repeat-Until`). Such invalid structures' DFDs are a mess. They can't even be Nassi-Schneiderman charted! (Again, that's one of the advantages of the N-S Chart: It renders these invalid structures impossible.) Such structures cause nothing but trouble. Never do this.

Avoid programs with this kind of flowchart with two exits, one of which is in the middle of the loop:

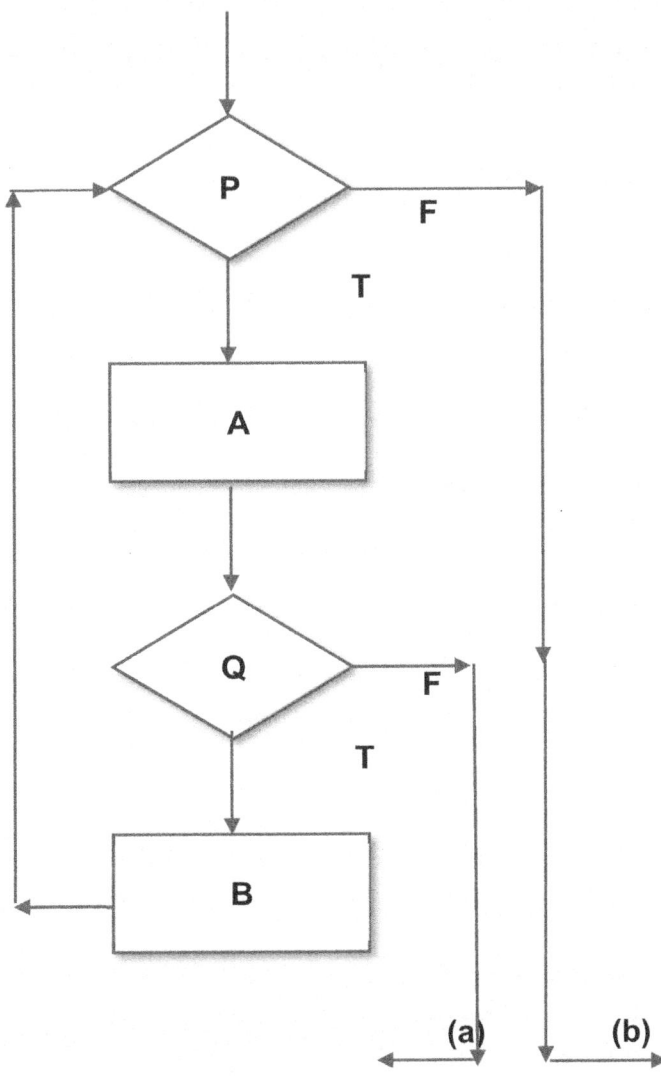

On Programming

This is very bad when exiting the **P** test and the **Q** test go to different locations (labeled (a) and (b) as shown here). It is also bad when they join up at the structure's exit and go to the same location (e.g., both to (a)).

Moral of the story: **Never exit out of the middle of a loop or have multiple loop exits**. It causes nothing but problems.

Instead of this mid-exit, two-exit loop, we *might* be able to use something like the following nested `While` loop. Note that the first test is **P'** ("P prime") instead of **P**. This is because if the **Q** test's `If`-structure bypasses block **B**, then the first **P'** test won't necessarily exit. It must test for **P** and for **Q**. But it won't be a simple **P AND Q** test because the first time through the loop we aren't supposed to test for **Q**. So, this isn't easy. No, it's better to avoid such a structure in any case.

Some programming languages (as noted above on p.79), have a built-in `Break` or `Exit-Loop` statement that does a mid-loop exit like this. Is that valid? It depends.

Many of them implement it via an invisible, embedded `If`-structure as we've done here. Implemented this way, it is useful and could be valid. However, from the outside, we can't tell how it is internally implemented, whether validly or not. But as our analysis shows, it isn't a good structure to use whether we code it ourselves or even if it's built in. Just avoid it. Better to be safe than sorry, especially when you're just starting out.

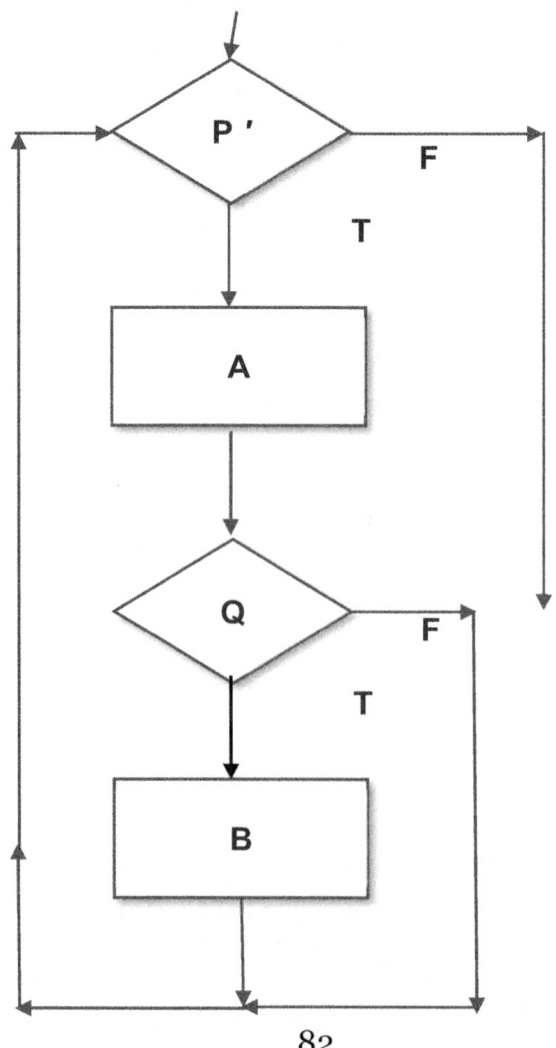

Unsafe Structures

Avoid **Do-While-Do**-*structured programs with this kind of flowchart with one exit in the middle:*

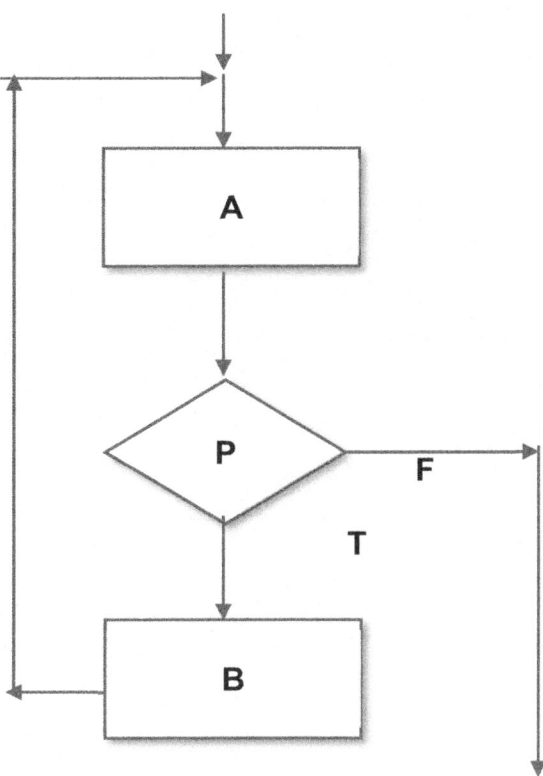

Again, **never exit out of the middle of a loop**. It causes nothing but problems.

Instead of this **Do-While-Do** loop, use the following nested **While** loop. Again note that the test is **P'** ("P prime") instead of **P** because by the time it is first executed, block **A** has already been executed once. If this were a counted loop and **P** was testing if the loop had been executed, say, 10 times, then **P'** would have to test for 9 times. What if it's not counted, but is testing some other occurrence? In that case, it isn't so easy. So it's better to avoid such a structure in any case. As above, it can be made valid, but it isn't easy and can have hidden problems.

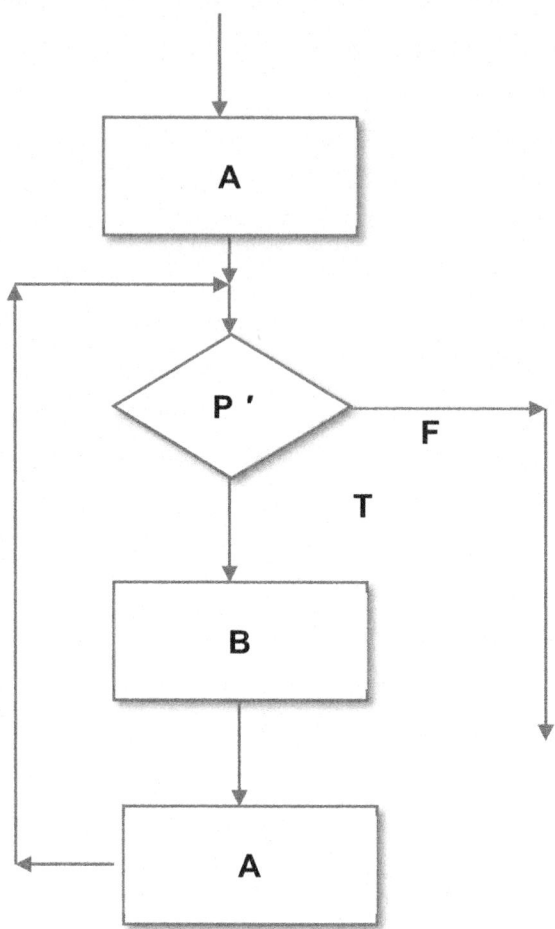

Unsafe Structures

And avoid this with two exits, one at each end:

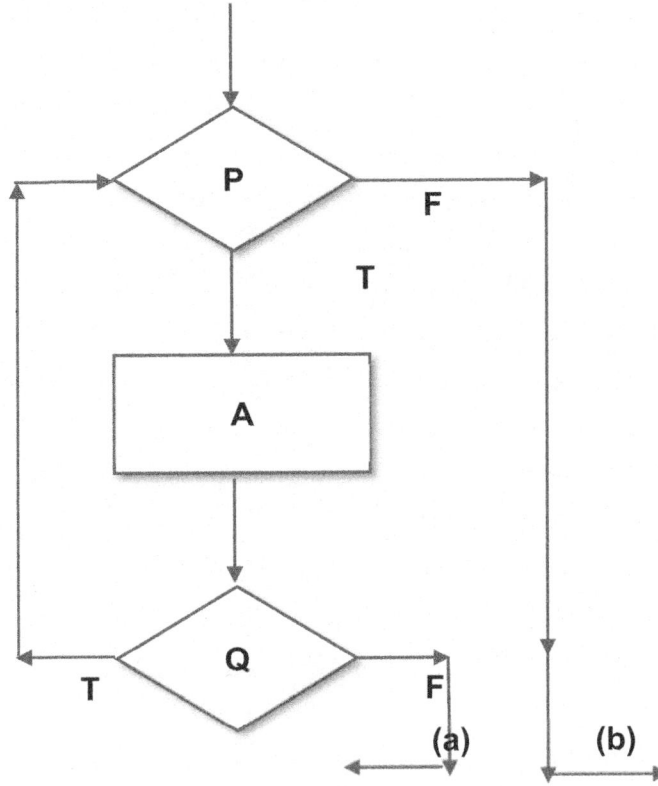

As above, this is bad when exiting the P test and the Q test go to different locations (again, (a) and (b) as shown here). It is also bad when they join up at the structure's exit and go to the same location.

It has similar problems to the above structures, so we won't go through the analysis.

Moral: **Never have two exits from a loop**. It causes nothing but problems.

And always *avoid having the flowlines go off to different destinations and never meet (see following chart). It really isn't even a structure, just a bunch of flowchart boxes:*

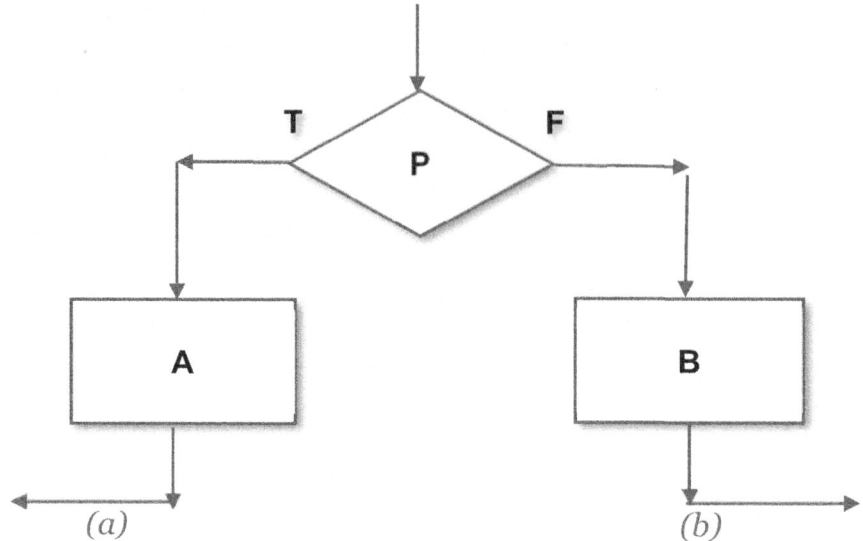

And never the twain shall meet again.

Unfortunately, this one is particularly easy to do in languages that include a `Go-To` statement. Fortunately, many modern languages omit the `Go-To`. Nevertheless, it can be done via other means in some other languages, also.

Moral: **Never have two exits from any structure**. It causes nothing but problems. Instead, if it involves an `If`-test, use a legitimate `If-Then-Else` (Conditional Execution) structure (pp. 33ff).

Sadly, all of these pseudo-structural errors are far too easy to do in many programming languages.

All such "structures" as these are *bad news*.

Conclusion

> *"Now this is not the end. It is not even the beginning of the end. But it is, perhaps, the end of the beginning."*
>
> *— Winston Churchill, 1942*

That's not the end of programming and that's not all there is to it. However, we've set a good foundation and have made a good beginning.

This should be enough to get started, headed in the right direction. And *that* is the main aim of this book – to get started in the *right* direction rather than the wrong directions that are often inadvertently foisted on the unsuspecting beginner.

Happy programming!

Enjoy!

What's next?

If you're bitten by the programming bug and want to pursue it more, I suggest starting by reading *Code Complete* by Steve McConnell and *The Pragmatic Programmer* by Dave Thomas and Andrew Hunt (see "Bibliographical Index", pp.139ff.

In fact, read almost anything by Steve McConnell, Fred Brooks, P. J. Plauger, John Bentley, Brian Kernighan, Watts Humphrey, and Harlan Mills.

Read lots of code.

Talk to experienced programmers. A lot. Find a mentor.

Take some classes.

Learn lots of techniques and methodologies, including object-oriented programming.

Learn lots of programming languages so you know the best tool for whatever problem you're presented with.

It'll help you code better to know how programming fits into the bigger picture. So learn something about related technologies and approaches like systems analysis, systems design, databases, software development life cycles, agile, testing, software engineering, implementation / installation, cyber-security, networks and networking, and so forth.

And **practice, practice, practice!**

On Programming

Appendix 1 – Conversion of Repeat-Until to and from Do-While

"Supply yourself with a mental equivalent, and the thing must come to you."

– *Emmet Fox*

Conversion of Repeat-Until to Sequence plus Do-While

We mentioned that the **Do-While** and **Repeat-Until** both accomplish iteration loops and can be converted into each other. For those who are interested, this first appendix shows how to do that conversion. It can be skipped by those who are not interested.

Consider first the **Repeat-Until** flowchart below, where P is such that we loop N times. (It needn't be a counted **For-Loop**, but the condition is such that it results in being executed N times.) Both P and A are executed N ties, and even if P were immediately true, A would get executed once anyway.

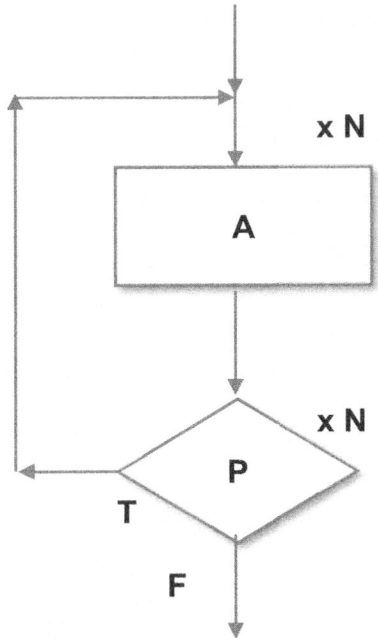
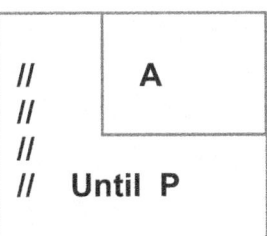

Now consider the **While** chart below. As is, this is not equivalent to the **Until**. The condition P ' ("P prime") in this case is ¬P (**not** P, the negation of the P in the previous chart). We choose this such that the condition is evaluated N tines. In everyday English, "Keep doing A until P" is similar to "While **not** P, continue doing A". But it isn't quite identical, since A will be executed N-1 times because the last evaluation of P ' will be false, which terminates the loop. Furthermore, if P' were immediately false, then A would never be executed at all. So far, that's not the same as the Until – in fact, it's short by one execution of A in all cases.

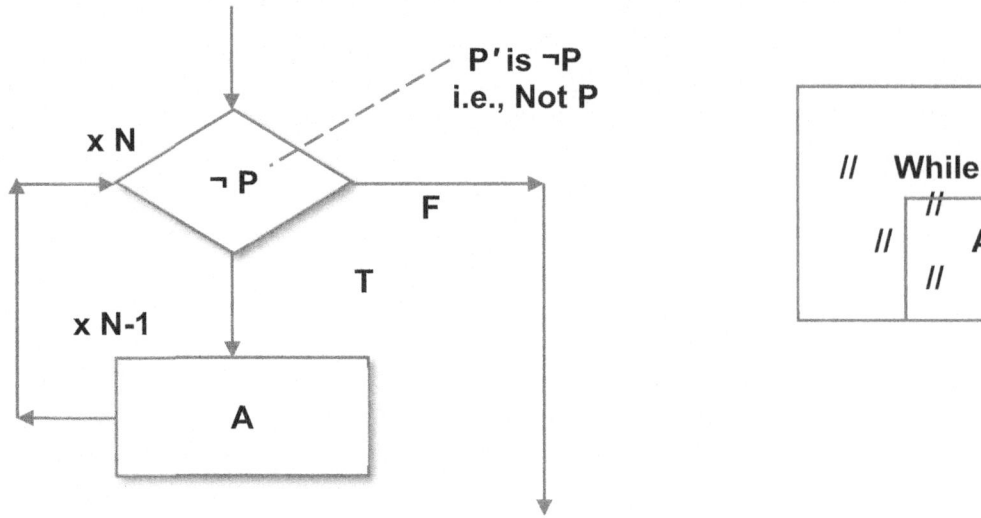

So, since we're short by one execution of A, all we need to do is take an extra copy of A and Sequence it on the front (or back) of the loop. It may be brute force, it works. Now the total number of times that A is executed is N as required. A is executed once in front of the loop. It is also executed N-1 times in the loop, while P' is still evaluated N times. This is identical to the Repeat-Until loop. Thus, an Until is equivalent to a While with another copy of the body sequenced in front of it. Or in pseudo-code, "Do A Until P" is equivalent to "A; While Not P Do A". They are different programs implementing the same function F.

We can verify the Sequence While program using the Sequence and While verification questions. (Try it yourself!) As noted, this is the easiest way to verify an Until: re-cast it as a Sequence and a While, and then verify that.

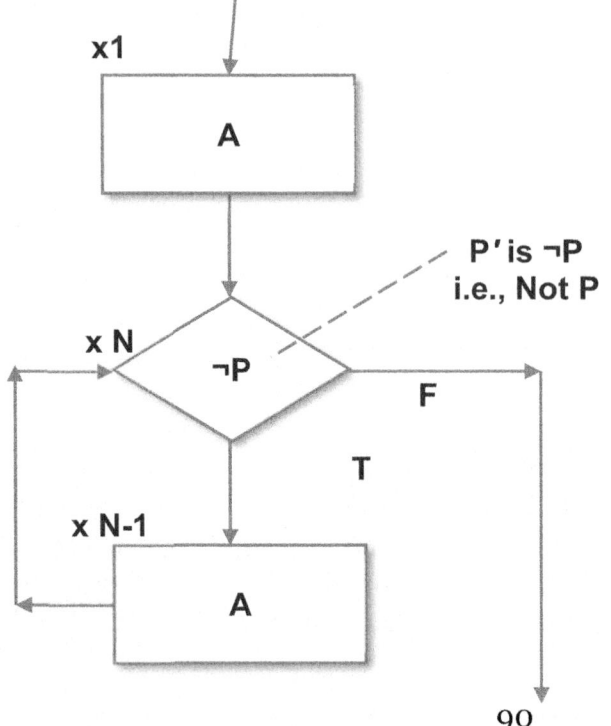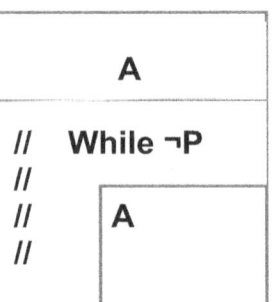

Appendix 1 – Conversion of Repeat-Until to and from Do-While

Conversion of Do-While into If-Then plus Repeat-Until

We can see by similar reasoning as above that we can also convert a `While` into an `Until`. (Details of the conversion are left to the reader as an exercise: Please try it!) In short, a `While` is equivalent to an `Until` embedded in an `If-Then`. While we won't go through the demonstration of this here, we will show the two equivalent flowcharts so that you can work through it and see it yourself.

The `While` loop:

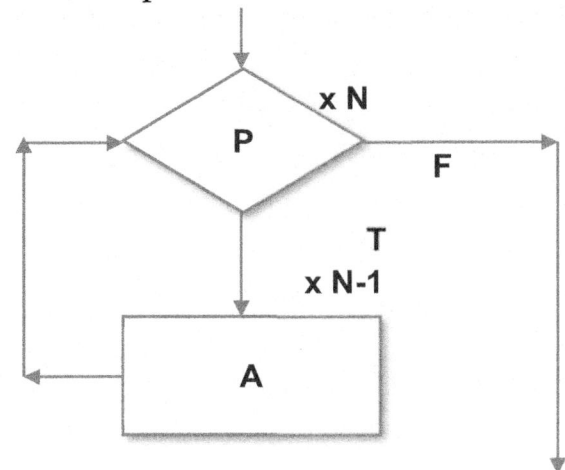
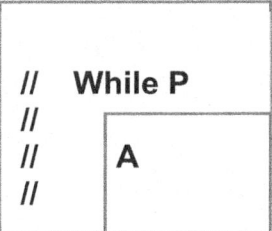

is equivalent to an `Until` loop embedded within an `If-Then`:

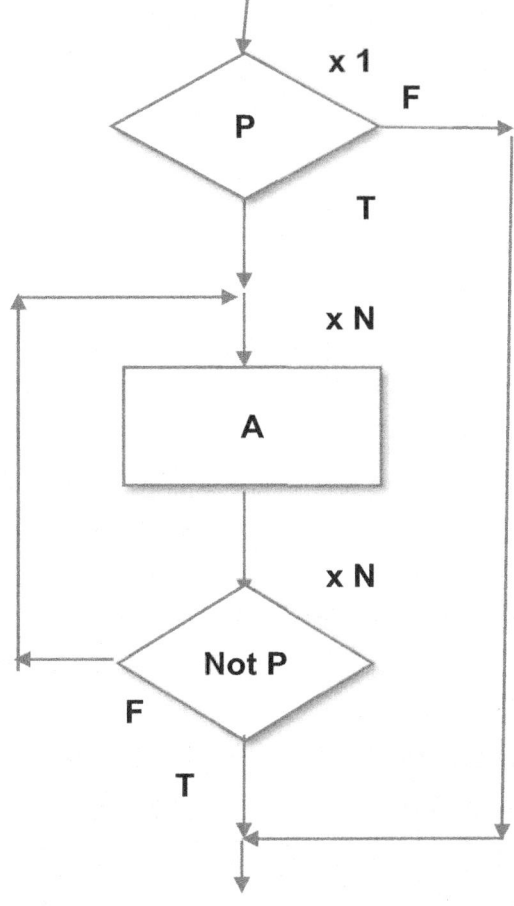
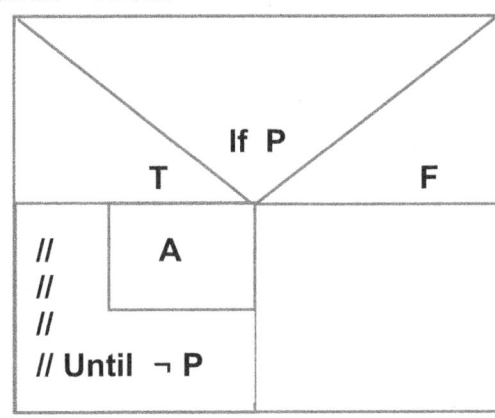

These are two versions of the same thing built using different control structures. The body `A` is executed the same number of times giving the same result. They are different programs implementing the same function `F`. If `P` causes immediate exit from the `Until` loop, it also causes immediate exit from the `If-Then` before the `While`. In pseudo-code, "`While P Do A`" is equivalent to "`If P Then Repeat A Until Not P`".

There is probably less use for turning a `While` into an `Until` like this. Nevertheless this shows that it can be done if it should prove necessary. I personally have found both equivalents most useful in day-to-day programming. They particularly seem to come in useful when constructing loops that read and process data in real production systems.

Appendix 2 – Variables, data types, and data structures

> *"I will, in fact, claim that the difference between a bad programmer and a good one is whether he considers his code or his data structures more important. Bad programmers worry about the code. Good programmers worry about data structures and their relationships."*
>
> – Linus Torvalds, Creator of Linux OS,
> message to "Gitl" mailing list, 27.Jun.2006

> *"Understanding what kind of data representations are needed for [real-] world programs takes practice."*
>
> – Matthias Felleisen, et al. 2018.
> in <u>How to Design Programs</u>

So far, the only kind of data that we've mentioned is simple "typeless" variables (see "Assignments and Variables", p.36). But it can get much more involved than that. So we have to know how our chosen programming language uses variables and data structures. Of course, since it varies from language to language, the details are beyond our present scope. Nevertheless, this is important, so a brief introduction is in order.

Data types

In most computer languages, data and variables can be of different <u>types</u>. This is similar to numbers in math – integers, "real" numbers (called "floating point" in programming languages), dates, text strings, and so forth. Wait, text strings? Math doesn't do that!

No, but computers do. We often think of computers as big, fast calculators, and of course they can do all that. Computers are actually general-purpose symbol manipulation machines (see "Appendix 6 – What is a computer?", p.129). They can do much more than math! Of course, when we think about it, we know this because we know that computers do word processing, handle personnel databases, do email, games, browse the Web, and many other things that aren't just calculating numbers.

The way most programming languages work, we can't store something of one data type in a variable of another data type. (That is, not without converting it first.) So, we could convert an integer `1` to a floating-point number `1.0`, for instance. Some languages do the conversions for us automatically. Others require us to use special built-in conversion functions (see "Subroutine", p. 77). To tell the compiler which data type we intend to use for each variable, we must code a <u>declaration</u>[44] statement. (This is usually called a `Declaration`, `Dimension`, or `Define` or some abbreviation thereof.) This tells the type and shape (more on that below) of the variable.

> Incidentally, when using a `Dimension` or similar statement to declare a variable type, it is best to add a line comment to the end of the statement. The comment should tell what the variable is and does. It should also include its units of measurement (if any). For instance, something like: `Dim Body_Temp as Integer [degrees F]` (where the square brackets indicate a comment in the notation we're using). Better still, name it something like `Body_Temperature_deg_F`. And *still* include a comment.

Not all programming languages deal with data types, however. They are called "<u>typeless</u>" languages. Pseudo-code doesn't deal with types either, so we don't use types here. Typeless languages don't have type declarations and do any needed conversions automatically. So, like pseudo-code, we don't have to concern ourselves with data types. Whew! What a relief! However, as you might expect, that comes with a downside also. Such languages usually aren't as powerful. They also are often much more limited in what they can do than languages in which we can specify exactly the kind and shape of our data. Worse, they make invalid assumptions about our data "behind the scenes". This can cause errors that are hard to find. When we explicitly declare our types and do our conversions ourselves, it's easier to find any type errors that may crop up.

Data Shape

We don't usually call it "shape", but that's pretty much what it is.

A simple variable is like one pigeonhole mailbox in a wall of mailboxes (see diagram below). It will store one thing, one value. But we can also have an <u>array</u>, like a row of pigeonholes, which can store several values. We address it (choose which one of the pigeonhole boxes) by specifying the name of the array (row) and the number of the box in the row (called a <u>subscript</u>). Like this: `Day(1)` or `Day(5)` or `Day(7)`, say. (Some languages use square brackets instead of parentheses. As always, they're each different.) We can use variables instead of numbers for the subscripts too. For example, `Day(N)` or `Account(X)`, where `N` and `X` are also variables representing numbers.

Before we can *use* an array, we must declare it or dimension it (see "Data types", above), telling the compiler its size and shape.

We can even have multi-dimensional arrays, which are like several (contiguous) rows of pigeonholes. We address them like this: `Pixel(5,10)`, or `Day(WeekNum, Weekday)`, or `Cell(Row, Column)`. Most languages can use more than two dimensions, too, as in `X(5, 3, 17)`.

---

[44] See "Internal Declarations", p.14 above.

Appendix 2 – Variables, data types, and data structures

Figure 4 – USPS post office boxes
(USPS photo, public domain)

Data structures

Some languages have complex data structures built in. With others, we build them ourselves by writing subroutines, functions, classes, or objects with their associated methods and properties. Some useful data structures include:

- <u>*Table*</u> – like a table or spreadsheet of data; much like an array (above) except that a table's columns are typically named instead of numbered, and perhaps most importantly, can each be of different data types (integer, floating point, text string, etc.). Tables often, but not always, can have a header row at the beginning that tells the names of the columns. An entire array, on the other hand (as above), is of a single data type (and its columns are typically not named but are numbered). Here's an example of a table:

Team	W	L	Pct	GB	Home	Away
Tampa Bay	48	20	.706		31-7	17-13
Baltimore	41	24	.631	5.5	20-12	21-12
NY	38	20	.567	9.5	21-17	17-12
Toronto	37	30	.522	10.5	19-13	18-17
Boston	33	33	.500	14	17-16	16-17

For examples of the use of a table data structure, see "Appendix 3 – More extended examples" (p.99 and following).

- *Stack* – like a stack of cafeteria plates, the last plate (or the last data) we put in, is the first we can take out (also called LIFO – Last In, First Out[45]).

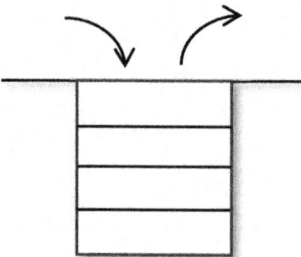

- *Queue* – like a line at a bank or grocery store, the first one in is the first one out (also called FIFO – First In, First Out).

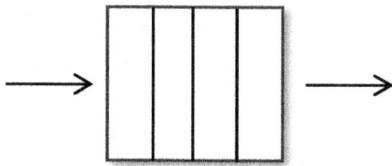

- *Linked list* – like a long, soft, flexible string of spaghetti with meatballs attached. A linked list can function similarly to a queue or other structures. However, its advantage is that data (meatballs) can be inserted (or deleted from) the middle, not just the end(s). (The "block chain" that Bitcoin is based on is essentially a glorified, distributed linked list.) There can also be doubly linked lists (block chain is one) where the links go both forward and backward.

The diagram here shows a singly linked list:

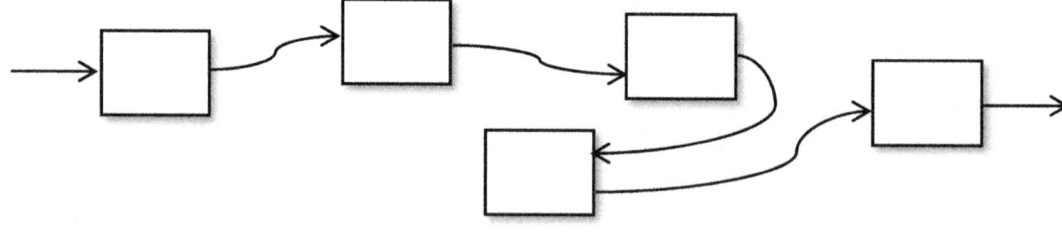

And here's a doubly-linked list:

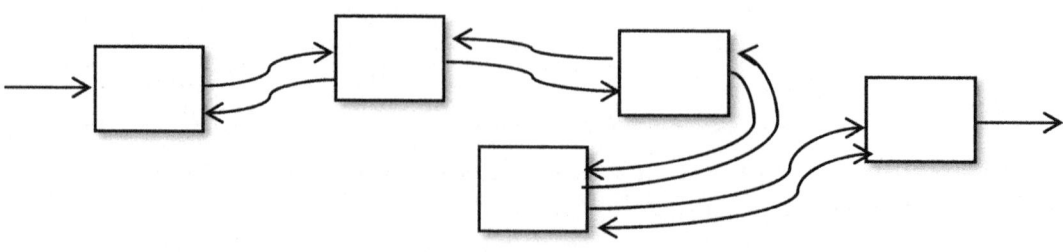

---

[45] Note that LIFO is not the same as First In, Last Out (FILO). Can you see why? FILO is rarely if ever used as a data structure. Can you tell why?

Appendix 2 – Variables, data types, and data structures

Adding a node to linked list: First, add the node by itself (anywhere):

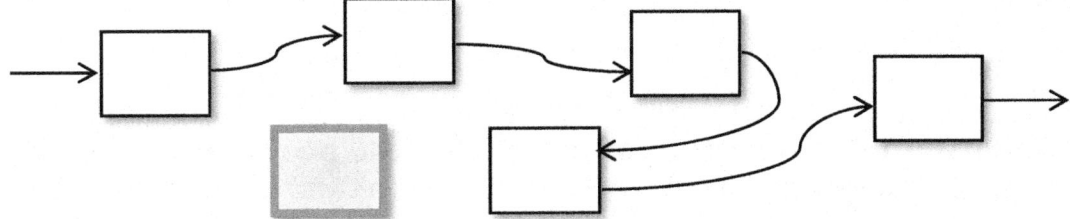

Then add a link from the new node to its new successor in the chain:

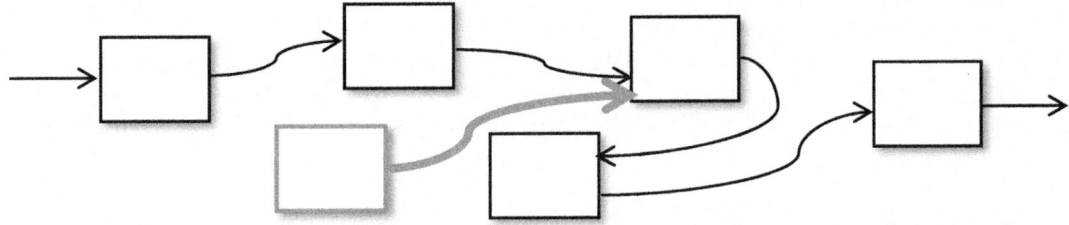

Finally, change the predecessor's link to point to the new node: Simple!

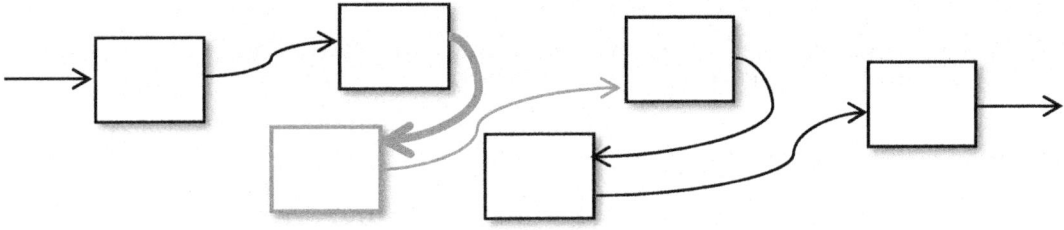

- *Tree* – like a family tree, the leaves of which are data blocks.

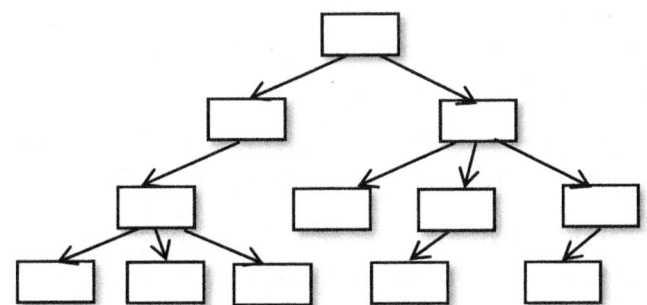

- *Object* – (Mentioned above, see "Object-oriented programming", p.7.) An object includes both a program (or "method") and its data (also called "attributes" or "properties"). Objects are often in "inheritable" hierarchies of formats, structures, classes, and/or actual data. A *class* can be viewed either as a program with its data, or as data with the programs that operate on it, or as a structure with its data attributes and program methods.

  An object is a particular instance of a specified class, inheriting its attributes and with specific data values of its own. Objects and classes are generally conceived of as models of something in the real world. Examples include buttons and boxes on a computer screen, turrets on an army tank or backhoe, cylinders or wheels on a car, and so forth. For this reason, object-oriented programming is in some ways more like modeling the problem domain than it is coding computer instructions.

- And of course, there are many, many more data structures.

The *data structure axiom* of programming emphasizing the importance of data structures is: **"Get the data structure right, and the program will write itself."** That may be a slight overstatement since programs don't write themselves! But it's not much of an exaggeration. In fact, the structure of the data generally will determine the way it is processed and therefore the structure of the program. In fact, some programming textbooks teach data structures before programming structures or commands.

As Dave Thomas and Andrew Hunt put it in *The Pragmatic Programmer*, "Programming is about code, but programs are about data". After all (as they again point out), "Programs are something that transform inputs into outputs". That's their very purpose.

Files and databases

All data we've discussed so far resides in RAM (random access memory – see "Von Neumann computer architecture", p.129). RAM is "volatile" and goes away when we turn off the computer (or even when we close the program). RAM is not only fast, but in addition to storing data, is the only place from which programs can be run or executed.

How, then, do we keep data around from day to day? We use files and databases.

A *file* is data stored on a hard disk drive, solid state drive, or other permanent storage. Such drives ae slower and less accessible than RAM, but are not volatile. Slower and less accessible than RAM, that is. Examples of files include word processing documents, spreadsheets, computer programs (when stored for future use and subsequent loading into RAM for execution), and generalized data of any sort.

Programming languages, or the operating systems they are run on, have special commands or built-in subroutines for accessing data stored in files.

Databases, on the other hand, are also stored on hard drives or permanent storage; but they are more structured. There are many different kinds and formats of databases. They might store their data as

- large tables (called "relational databases", probably the most common format today),
- hierarchical trees,
- linked lists, or
- in other formats.

Databases are accessed either via special subroutines in a database management system (*DBMS*) or via special database languages such as *SQL* (the Structured Query Language). Such database languages may either be separate from our normal programming language or integrated in as part of the language itself.

Appendix 3 – More extended examples

> *"Brethren, join in following my example, and observe those who walk according to the pattern you have in us."*
>
> – <u>Philippians 3:17</u> *(NASB1995)*

These programs are examples of what I call "recreational programming". I didn't actually need to use them as utilities (or vary rarely, in any case). Rather, I did them both to learn and because they were fun. And, of course, I did them to share as examples.

KWIC Index

Another extended example: Suppose we wanted to write a program to produce a Keyword In Context (KWIC) index of all the words in a document. Well, let's index only the *relevant* words, omitting stop words. (*Stop words* are short words like *a, the, by, for, has, or, to, was, we,* and so forth, that are never put into an index.)

The distinction of a KWIC index is that it includes the line of text along with each word that is indexed. The index line is formatted so that the indexed words all line up in a column in the middle. Some concordances of the Bible do this. In this example from *Strong's Concordance* (1890; public domain), the italicized letter in each line represents the indexed word. Part of the sentence in which it occurs is shown.

```
TODAY
    glorious was the king of Israel t ............. 2Sa 6:20
    T thy servant knoweth that I have ......... 2Sa 14:22
    T shall the house of Israel .................... 2Sa 16:3
TOE
    upon the great t of their right ............... Ex 29:20     931
    upon the great t of his right ................. Lev 8:23     931
    upon the great t of his right ................. Lev 14:14    931
    upon the great t of his right ................. Lev 14:17    931
    upon the great t of his right ................. Lev 14:25    931
    upon the great t of his right ................. Lev 14:28    931
TOES
    upon the great t of their right ............... Lev 8:24     931
    cut off his thumbs and his great t .. Judg 1:6          931,7272
    thumbs and their great t cut off ..... Judg 1:7          931,7272
    fingers, and on every foot six t .............. 2Sa 21:20    676
    t were four and twenty, six on ................ 1Chr 20:6    676
    whereas thou sawest the feet and t ........ Dan 2:41     677
    as the t of the feet were part of ............ Dan 2:42     677
TOGARMAH (to-gar'-mah) A son of Gomer.
    Ashkenaz, and Riphath, and T ............. Gen 10:3     8425
    Ashchenaz, and Riphath, and T ........... 1Chr 1:6     8425
    They of the house of T traded in .......... Eze 27:14    8425
    the house of T of the north ................... Eze 38:6     8425
```

Figure 5 – KWIC index in Strong's Concordance
(1890, public domain)

Here's an example using some of the text of this present book:

Part of the line before the word	Indexed Word	Part of the line after the word
the for-each structure mentioned	ABOVE	we could also have used a
-termine whether the "word" Wd is	ACTUALLY	only punctuation. on the
separate "words", then we might	ADD	a **t**hird part to the conditional
the same way: by checking word Wd	AGAINST	a list of punctuation.
at it includes the line of text	ALONG	with each word that is indexed
the number of the word). we're	ASSUMING	that our system or language
the for-each method). we're also	ASSUMING	that the system can provide
he middle. Initial high-level	BLOCK	diagram
such a string search will be	BUILT	into essentially any and all
short words should handle that	CASE	so we probably won't need a th
punctuation. On the other hand,	CHECK	for short words should handle
we'd do it the same way: by	CHECKING	word W against a list of punc
indexed words all line up in a	COLUMN	in the middle. Initial high
each condition, or by a single	COMPOUND	condition as here. If our

Appendix 3 – More extended examples

Initial high-level block diagram

Here's our initial high-level block diagram of the program:

Setup and Initialize
Process each word in document, building `Words_Data` **table**
Write `Words_Data` **table to** `temp_file`
Sort `Temp_File` **by** `Word` **column (use built-in system sort)**
Add file headers, if needed
Display, open, or print, if needed
Clean-up and quit

Next level decomposition and expansion

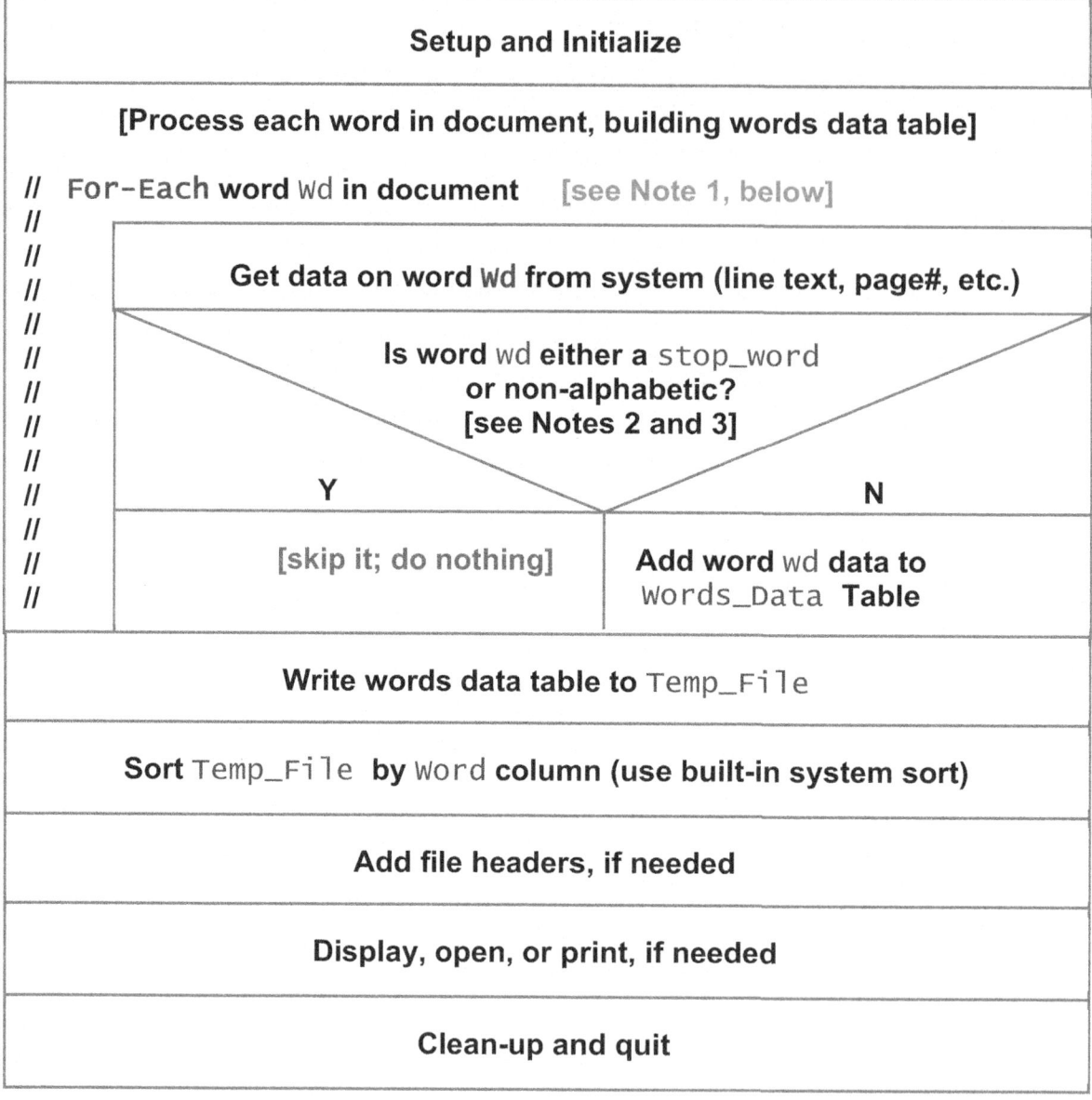

Note 1: Here, we're using the For-<u>Each</u> structure mentioned above (p.73). We could also have used a counted For-Loop like this:

```
For Word_Num = 1 to Number_of_words_in_document; wd = Word(Word_Num); ... and so forth.
```

Either way, wd represents the text of the word itself (not the occurrence number of the word). We're assuming that our system (or programming language) can tell us how many words are in the document (in the For-Loop method). Or alternatively that it can extract the next word for us (in the For-Each method). We're also assuming that the system can provide data on the word: the full text string of the line it's in, the page and line number, etc. How it does this is unique to each system and language.

Note 2: The condition in the first `If-Then-Else`, here, is a compound condition. If *either* the word `wd` is short *or* if it is a stop word, then skip it. This might be implemented by nesting two separate `If-Then-Else` structures, one for each condition as below. Or it could be done by a single compound condition as above.

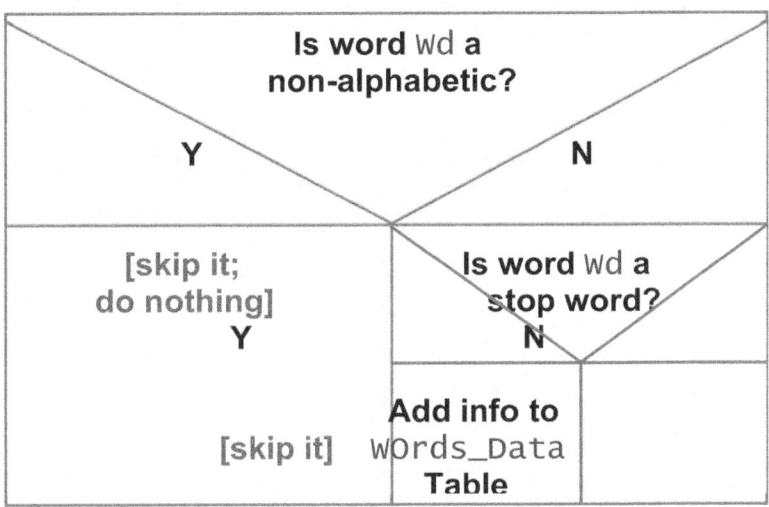

Suppose our language treats punctuation as separate "words". Then we might add a third part to the conditional to determine whether the "word" `wd` is only punctuation. But checking for short words should handle that case, so we probably won't need a third part to the conditional.

Note 3: Let's say our data structure will have the stop words listed in a text string list. Then all we need to do is to see whether word `wd` is contained in the `Stop_Words` string. Such a string search capability is built into essentially all programming language(s). If we had to check for punctuation as "words", we'd do it the same way: by checking word `wd` against a list of punctuation.

Words_Data table

The word and context data from the system will likely arrive via individual variables retrieved from the system's Application Programming Interface (*API*). We will store them in a table data structure (see "table" Data structures, p.95) for use in the rest of the program.

(It might be better and faster to do this in some other manner. We're using a table here to illustrate the table data structure mentioned above. More on this, below.)

Here's what our `Words_Data` table looks like, with some sample data filled in. It will be initialized and built in the order that the words occur in the document. However, that is not how we want them sorted in the final KWIC index, so we'll have to something about that.

Item Number	Word text	Word_Count	Page_Number	Line_Number	Line text
1	Another	1	1	1	As another extended example...
2	Extended	2	1	1	As another extended example ...
3	Example	3	1	1	As another extended example ...
4	Suppose	4	1	1	As another extended example suppose ...
⋮	⋮	⋮	⋮	⋮	⋮
52	Condition	1	3	14	One for each condition ...
75	Condition	2	2	5	is a compound condition if either ..
212	Condition	3	2	10	The condition in the first if-then-else...

Item Number is the word number in the document and the row number for accessing the table. For instance, *Item Number* N is the N-th word in the document and the N-th row in the table. *Item Number* is not a column of the table, as are the rest below, but is just how we index or access the table.

Word text is the word we've found (i.e., wd).

Word_Count is the number of occurrences of that word, or the number of this occurrence of it. Many words will occur more than once in the document; this tells how many so far.

Page_Number is the page number this occurrence of the word is found on.

Line_Number is the line of that page that the word is found on.

Line text is the full text of the entire line, including the given word.

There will be a row in the table for each word in the document.

Appendix 3 – More extended examples

Decomposition and expansion of the second major loop

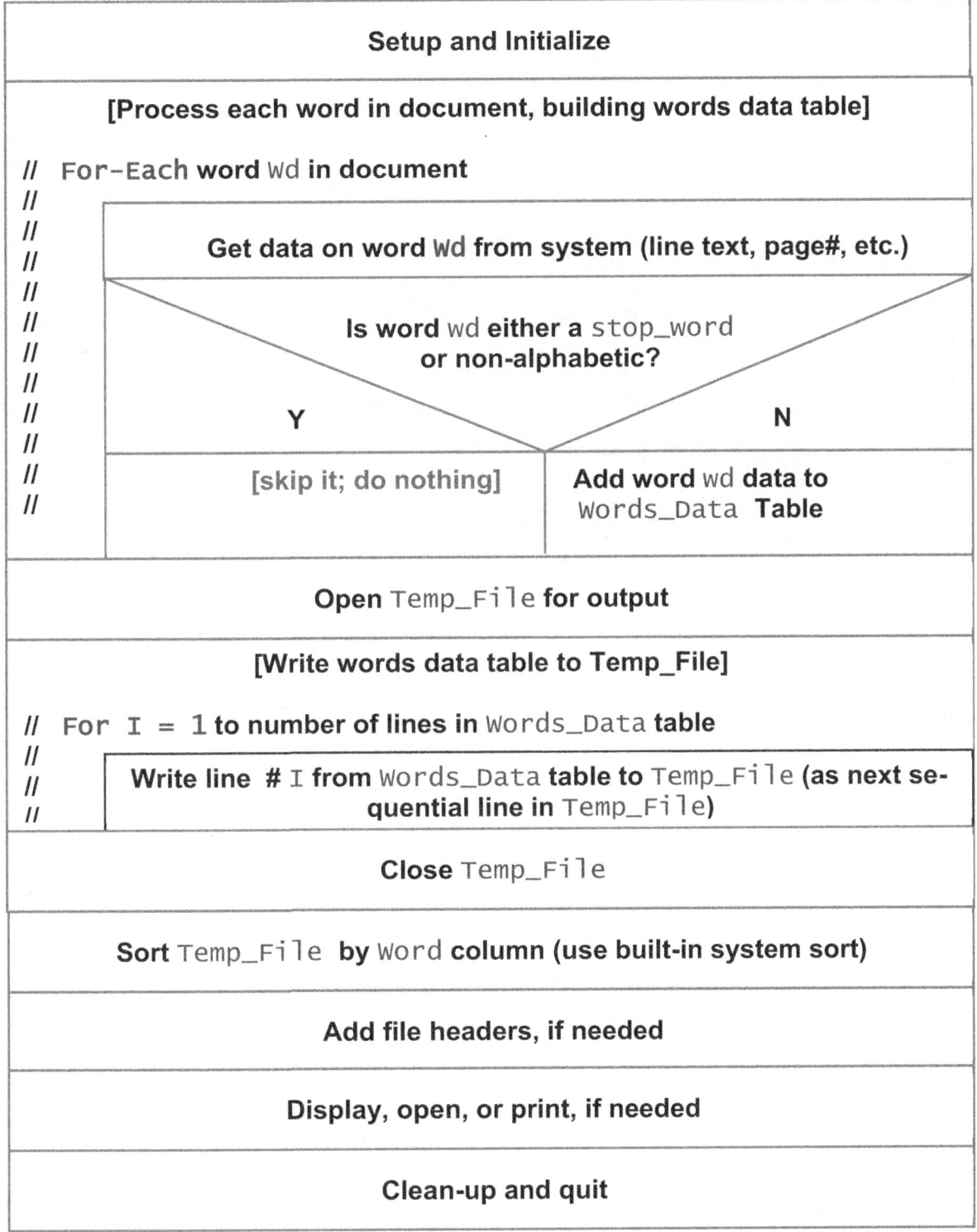

That's it! We're done, at least for now. We call a built-in system sort to do the sorting. We're not worrying about file headers or displaying, opening, or printing it because these are all system- and language-dependent and so are beyond the scope of this book. We'll do them the way our system and language require. Suffice it to say that we will be able to do that. (Again, confidence and faith.)

Questions

Can you write a flowchart for this program? (That is left to the reader as an exercise[46].)

More importantly, can you think of a better way to do this? Perhaps a more efficient way?

What about omitting the `Word_Data` table and writing directly to the `Temp_File`? Is there any reason we couldn't do that?

That would be a good idea. We used the intermediate `Word_Data` table to illustrate a little about table data structures and their processing. That probably isn't necessary. Writing to an intermediate `Temp_File`, however, is necessary. That's because we need to sort the output using a built-in system sort. That's the best and fastest way to sort, but it sorts files not internal data structures like arrays. So we do have to write our output data to an intermediate `Temp_File`.

It would be good if we could figure out *something* to do to improve the speed of processing. This program runs very slowly, though not so much because of that intermediate data table. Rather, its slow because we're going through every single word in the document. At this point in my writing, this book is about 25,000 words long, so that would be a lot of words to go through. I ran KWIC against a 1000-word extract and even that took quite a long time to process.

Things that run on the *order of magnitude*[47] of N (where in our case N is the number of words in the document) – $\mathcal{O}(N)$ as we say in "big-O" notation – are slow. Things that run on the order of N squared – $\mathcal{O}(N^2)$ – are *very* much slower than that. Sometimes a loop within a loop will be $\mathcal{O}(N^2)$, so that's something to watch out for.

Merging the two loops as mentioned above would speed it up a little, but it would still be $\mathcal{O}(N)$, so it would still be slow.

What else could we do to improve this? Can you think of anything?

That's left to the reader as an exercise, because frankly, I haven't thought it through yet, myself. In a sense, it doesn't matter much because I rarely need to use this program. It might not be worth the time to optimize it compared to the few times I run it. (That's a tip about efficiency and *optimization*, too, by the way: Don't waste time optimizing what doesn't need optimization! And don't optimize while you're initially developing the

---

[46] In fact, all the questions are thought-questions to be pondered and considered. There are no answers in the back of the book (I checked).

[47] *Order of magnitude* is essentially the exponent of a number or, put another way, the number of places or zeroes to the left of the decimal point (plus or minus 1/3 or so). So, 1000 is $\mathcal{O}(3)$, as is 2000, 3000, 900, etc. 1,000,000 is $\mathcal{O}(6)$, as is 2,000,000 and 700,000 and so forth.

Appendix 3 – More extended examples

program. Find out later what, if anything, needs to be optimized and why, then optimize only that.)

If we need to create KWIC indexes of documents very often, or if we need to make a KWIC index of a very large and critical document, it would be best to see if there's a commercial KWIC-indexer program available. As with sorting, it will probably be much more efficient and worthwhile to use a KWIC system or third-party utility.

Nevertheless, this has served its purpose as a good illustration.

Table-driven Finite State Machine (FSM)

Intended for advanced readers. Feel free to skip this if you're not interested.

A *Finite State Machine* (*FSM*), for our purposes, is an event-processing program or a software simulation of a physical process driven by events. It defines what the program (or system) is supposed to do when certain events occur. The action taken depends on both which event occurs and on what state the "machine" is in at the time.

Wikipedia uses the example of a subway turnstile: If we push the turnstile when it's locked, nothing happens. If we put a coin, token, or farecard in the slot first, it unlocks it so that a push will open it. (Of course, it requires enough coins to cover the fare before it unlocks.) Then, having been pushed, it reverts to the locked state so that nobody else can enter after us.

Here is a simplified state-transition diagram of that turnstile FSM:

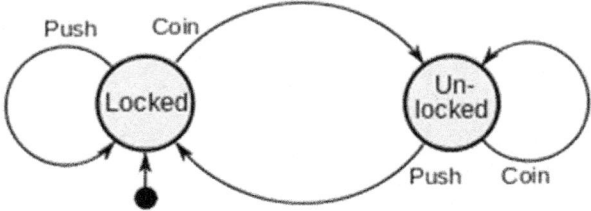

Figure 6 – Subway turnstile finite state machine
(Chetvorno, Public domain CC-0, Wikipedia)

The arcs represent the events or conditions and the transitions between states. The circles represent the states and the action or processing that takes place in that state. It is useful and illustrative to draw FSMs as state-transition (or condition-action) diagrams. But they are usually implemented in software using tables.

Suppose we need to parse input lines from a file of assignments and due dates. We want to produce a list of what's due today, due tomorrow, and overdue. (This is something that we wouldn't program "in real life". It is built into all calendar systems, day planner apps, and the like. Nevertheless, it's still a good example.)

Our FSM will parse each line, looking for **Tab** characters that delimit the fields. When we hit a **Tab**, we start a new field. When we hit another **Tab**, the first field is ended and we save it and begin another field. We ignore runs of multiple **Tabs**. When we hit the end of the line, we save the field we're in and quit.

State-transition diagram

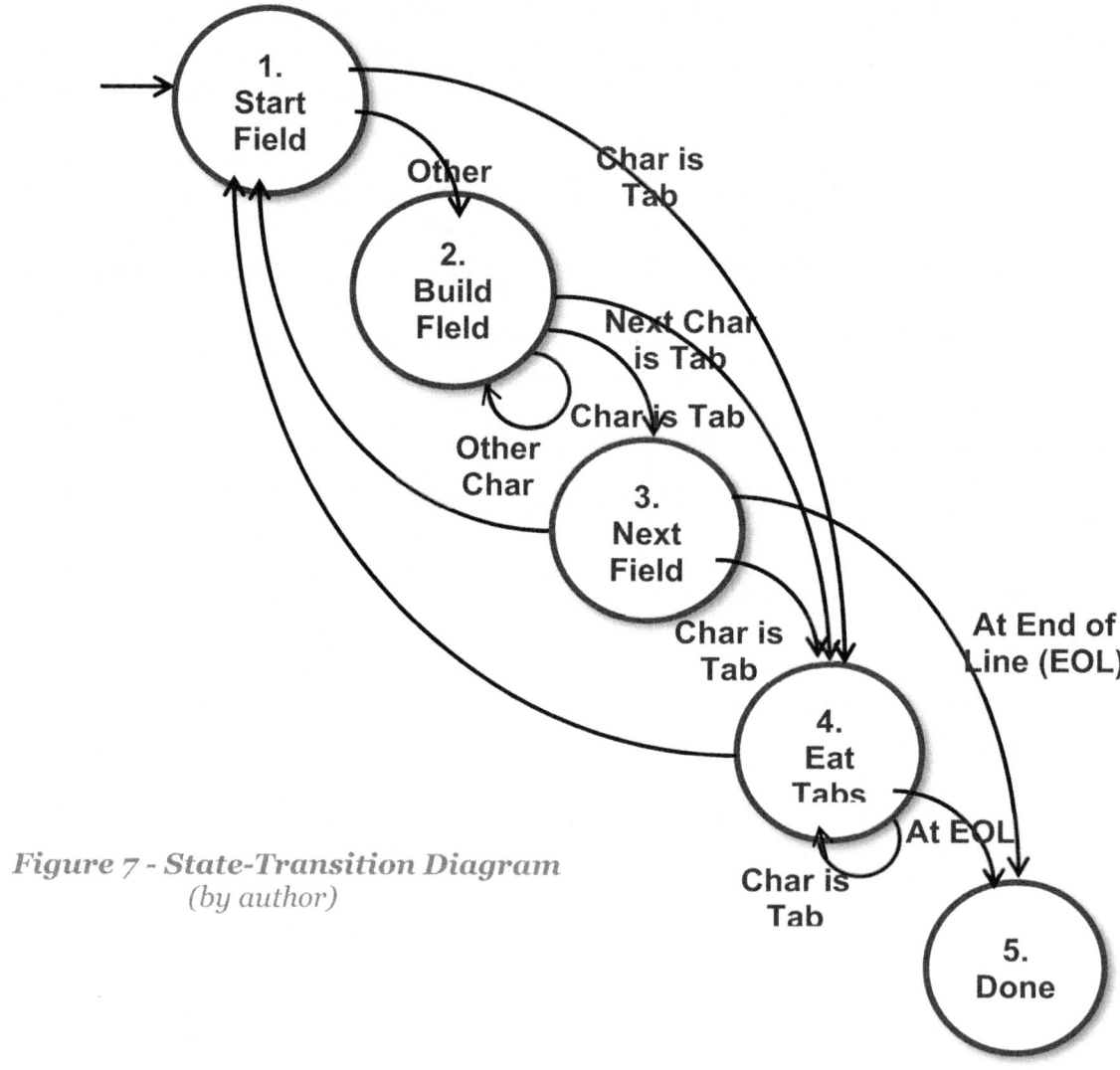

Figure 7 - State-Transition Diagram
(by author)

Does it remind you of Figure 3 - Fundamental Programming Algorithm on p. 17? That was a state-transition diagram, too!

This is complex looking for a relatively simple sounding problem! But the state-transition table below will be simpler (and that's what our program will be based on). However, we usually need to first draw the diagram to figure out the table.

What's more, though the problem statement sounds simple, doing it without an FSM is usually more difficult and complex and more error prone. Without an FSM, it would be a bigger program, involving a lot more **If-Then-Else** conditions, intermediate data variables, and opportunities to get things wrong.

Appendix 3 – More extended examples

State-transition table

Condition → State ↓	1. Current Character is Tab	2. Next Character is Tab (looking ahead)	3. Other Character (not Tab)	4. At End of Line
1. Start Field	to 4-Eat Tabs		to 2-Build Field	
2. Build Field	to 3-Next Field		Add character to Field name; *and* stay in state 2-Build Field;	
3. Next Field	to 4-Eat Tabs	to 4-Eat Tabs	to 1-Start [new] Field	to 5-Done
4. Eat Tabs	Stay in state 4-Eat Tabs	to 4-Eat Tabs	to 1-Start [new] Field	to 5-Done
5. Done				

This is a two-dimensional array (see "arrays" in "Data Shape", p.94). So we address it as `ST_Table(x, y)` or more accurately `ST_Table(State, Condition)`. So, `ST_Table(1, 3)` or `ST_Table(Start_Field, Other_Char)` is 2 or `Build_Field`. This means that if we're in state 1, `Start_Field` and we get another non-`Tab` character, then we transition to state 2, `Build_Field`.

The first line of the table, for example, says that if we're in the `Start_Field` state and get a `Tab` character, then we move to the `Eat_Tabs` state and see what happens next. But if we get another *non-*`Tab` character in that `Start_Field` state, then (as noted above) we move to the `Build_Field` state and see what happens *then*.

The second line says that if we get that same `Tab` character while we're in the `Build_Field` state, then we transition to the `Next_Field` state. But if we get a *non-*`Tab` character while in the `Build_Field`, then we add that character to the field name that we're building and then stay in the `Build_Field` state to see what happens next.

Can you tell what happens in the other lines of the table?

What happens when the table cells are blank? They are situations that should never occur ("should" being the operative word). We'd include them in our program as an error state. That is, if they ever occur, we will call an error-handling routine or subroutine.

By the way, do you notice what we've omitted in this? For one thing, it doesn't include reading the lines of the input file (schedule file). That's because that is outside of, and has nothing to do with, processing the fields within an input line. Our overall *program* must handle Input and Output (*I/O*), but our FSM only handles identifying and processing the characters of the line into fields since it's only *part* of the overall program. But there's more that's missing. Think about what it might be. We'll discuss this, below.

Top-level diagram

Setup and Initialize
Process each line in input schedule file, parsing each line with our FSM to identify date fields and associated schedule event names
Clean-up and quit

Appendix 3 – More extended examples

Next-level breakdown, including the FSM

Setup and Initialize
[Process each line in input schedule file, parsing each line with our FSM to identify date fields and associated schedule event names] `//` **while not End of File** (EOF) `//` `//` ┌───┐ `//` │ **Read input line from schedule file** │ `//` ├───┤ `//` │ **Use FSM to identify fields on line** │ `//` ├───┤ `//` │ **If date matches (i.e., Today, plus or minus), then display matching line with date and schedule event** │ `//` └───┘
Clean-up and quit

Next level of decomposition / expansion

Setup and Initialize

[Process each line in input schedule file, parsing each line with our FSM to identify date fields and associated schedule event names]

```
// While not End of File (EOF)
//
//        Read input line from schedule file
//
//        [Use FSM to identify fields on line]
//
//        For C = 1 to number of characters on line
//
//              Determine Condition [character type] matching character C
//              [This might be done using a Select-Case structure, but I
//              won't detail it here; it's left to the reader as an exercise]
//
//              If State = 2 (i.e, Build_Field) and Condition
//                     = 3 (i.e., Other Non-Tab Char)
//                     [see Note 1 below]
//
//              Y                                          N
//
//              Data_Field ← Data_Field        [skip it; do nothing]
//              & character C
//              [I.e, append character
//              to Data_Field)
//
//              Next_State ← ST_Table(Current_State, Con-
//              dition)
//
//              If Data_Field is a date,
//              then Date_Field ← Data_Field
//              [see Note 2 below]
//
//        If Date_Field = Today then display entire input line
//        [see Note 3 be[low]
```

Clean-up and quit

Appendix 3 – More extended examples

Note 1: Only `state(2, 3)`, `Build_Field` getting another non-`Tab` character, has a processing action (other than a state transition). So we're using a simple `If-Then-Else` structure to handle it. If many cells in our state-transition table also had associated processing actions, then we could use a `Select-Case` structure. More likely, we'd use a table structure that specifies the processing action (perhaps via a subroutine call). For instance, the processing action could be specified in a separate third table dimension or even a separate table. But that is not necessary here.

Note 2: Again, this is an `If-Then-Else` structure which we are now very familiar with. So its expansion and detailing is left to the reader as an exercise.

Note 3: Another `If-Then-Else` structure, this time involving I/O, which is language- and system-specific and is therefore beyond the scope of this book.

Questions

What other problems or programs might be susceptible to a finite state machine type of implementation? As noted, it may seem complex, but it simplifies things *considerably* compared to the more tedious and complex alternatives. There are many problems that an FSM can clarify or simplify either in concept or in actual application and implementation. You might consider it next time you run into a complex problem.

Could we implement a finite state machine as an event-triggered collection of objects with their associated methods and properties? (Perhaps the states would be the objects.) Why or why not? Consider and ponder it as we look at another example.

Event-driven interactive Tic-Tac-Toe

We're all familiar with the simple childhood tic-tac-toe game (known as "noughts and crosses", in Britain). This example is a sketch of an object-oriented (or at least *semi*-object-oriented) program to play tic-tac-toe with the computer.

It displays a standard 3x3 tic-tac-toe grid. Each square of the grid is an invisible "button". When it is clicked by the user, it changes the square from blank to "X". Then the computer takes its turn, responding to the move by making its own move with "O". (There is also an option for the computer to move first.) When three Xs or Os are in a row, the game terminates and the system declares the winner.

In object-oriented programming terms, the nine cells of the 3x3 board are the "objects". (Technically, each of the 9 buttons would be a separate object instance of a single generic cell class – see "class", p.97, above.) When activated (clicked), they run the "method" program for a cell. The method, in turn, runs a subroutine to determine the computer's move and then updates the display of the board. (Technically, the 3x3 grid display itself would also be an object, but since it is not active or clickable and does nothing, we will ignore that distinction for now.)

The data structure is a 3x3 array (see "arrays", p.94) corresponding to the 3x3 grid that will be displayed. Each element of the array can be "X", "O", or blank. This, and several other state- and status-related variables may be "public" or "global": They are shared and accessible to all our tic-tac-toe subprograms. (In another style of object-oriented programming, we could have them be owned by and subordinate to the 3x3 grid object. Or owned by the cell objects themselves. While that might be better, we'll have them public, global, and in a sense owned by the main program, for now.)

Because the details of an object-oriented system are heavily programming language dependent, we will keep this program design at a high level to "abstract" them out (i.e., ignore them). We will also "abstract out" the rather tedious details of the logic to determine the next move – but then, we all intuitively know those details anyway since we do them every time we play tic-tac-toe ourselves!

The tic-tac-toe system, then consists of several subprograms:

- Main – The main control program
- StartFresh – Initialization (and reinitialization)
- NextMove – Move-logic "engine" to generate the computer's next move. This is automatically called by the O-O system when a grid cell "button" is clicked. (So we do not see a "`call`" statement for it in our program.) Put another way, clicking a grid cell button causes an event that the O-O system handles. It handles it by invoking the method program for the object associated with that cell/button.
- UpdateGrid – Update the 3x3 grid "game board" in its current status of Xs and Os for display by the system. (If we implemented this differently, we might not need to do this, but it's useful to see how to do it this way.)
- CheckWin – Check whether the move just made was a winning move (three in a row)

Unlike the above examples which we built up step by step, we present this one only once in its complete (though relatively high level) form. It seems too confusing to show the step-by-step construction of several subprograms. And since we all know how tic-tac-toe works, it seems unnecessary.

Appendix 3 – More extended examples

Main

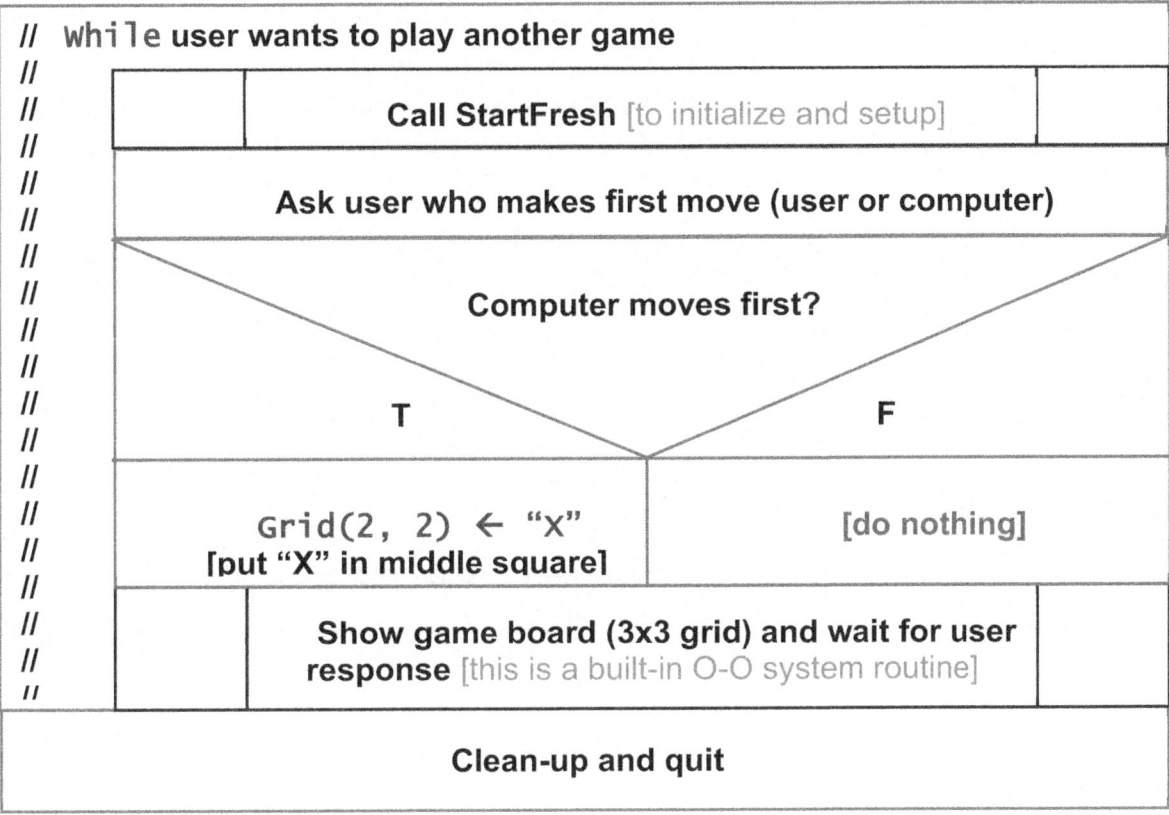

StartFresh

StartFresh simply consists of two nested `For-Loop`s that go through the 3x3 grid and reset it to blanks. It also resets the shared `Win` global variable to indicate that nobody has won yet.

```
// For X = 1 to 3
//
//      // For Y = 1 to 3
//      //
//      //      Grid(X, Y) ← blank
//
//      Win ← null
```

NextMove

	\tCall CheckWin [to see if anyone's won yet]			
	Lengthy If-Then-Else structure to evaluate grid [see Note 1]			
	If user wins	If we can win	If we can block	Otherwise
[do nothing]	Chose cell that wins		Choose cell that blocks	Choose random cell
	Call CheckWin [re-evaluate if that leads to a win; See Note 2]			
	Call UpdateGrid [to format and then display the 3x3 grid]			

Note 1: For compactness at a high level, I've diagrammed this using the N-S symbol for a `Select-Case` structure. However, the actual structure is a long `If-Then`-multiple`Else` structure. That structure evaluates different slices of the 3x3 grid in each `Else-If` clause. (A `Select-Case` structure, on the other hand, evaluates a single condition, comparing to multiple possible outcomes. That is not what we need here.)

Note 2: We've checked for a win both before and after our move logic. Is this necessary? Why? If it isn't necessary, we could speed things up a bit by eliminating one pass through the grid. But since it's only a 9-cell grid, any speedup would be minor at best.

UpdateGrid

	Reflect `Grid(X,Y)` **data structure in game board grid Object** [see Note 3]
	Call built-in O-O system routine to show game board and wait for user response

Note 3: In this particular implementation, the internal representation of the 3x3 tic-tac-toe grid is a simple 3x3 array (see "arrays", p.94 above. Yet the clickable display is a different kind of object. Consequently, we need to reflect the Grid in the Object and that's what this routine really does. If we'd implemented it differently, with different data structures, then perhaps they could have been one and the same. In that case, updating the grid would be the same as displaying the clickable board object. But in this implementation, alas, that was not to be.

Appendix 3 – More extended examples

CheckWin

> **An 8-part `If-Then-ElseIf` structure to check the 8 possible winning combinations** [see Note 4]

Note 4: Here, it's been implemented as an 8-part `If-Then-ElseIf` structure. Could we do it via `For-Loops`? Could we use a different data structure to improve this? Would it be worth it if we did?

Questions

The move logic engine is very tedious, consisting of dozens of `Else-If` clauses in a very long `If-Then-Else` structure. Can you think of a simpler way, perhaps by using a different data structure than our 3x3 array? Or for that matter, by any other method to simplify it or make it more elegant?

Since the grid consists of only 9 cells, it may be that we can't do much to speed things up. For such a small grid, the speed will be pretty good for something this small, anyway. Or, since the move logic is so tedious, maybe we can. But even if we can't increase the speed, maybe we can simplify things, make them clearer, and more elegant.

This implementation of Tic-Tac-Toe is event-driven and on some level utilizes objects. Is it truly object-oriented? Why or why not? That's an unfair question, as it's beyond the scope of this book. Nevertheless, considering what you know already, it's worth pondering.

Think about these things.

On Programming

Appendix 4 – Loop Invariants

> *"The secret of success is constancy to purpose."*
>
> – Benjamin Disraeli

Intended for advanced readers. Feel free to skip this if you're not interested.

As alluded to above (p.46), "A *loop invariant* is a property of a program loop that is true before (and after) each iteration. It is a logical assertion, sometimes checked within the code by an assertion call. Knowing its invariant(s) is essential in understanding the effect of a loop. ... From a programming methodology viewpoint, the loop invariant can be viewed as a more abstract specification of the loop, which characterizes the deeper purpose of the loop beyond the details of this implementation." (Wikipedia)

At first, that almost sounds pointless. It seems as though almost anything could be invariant and not change with the iterations of a loop. By this overly simplistic definition, a loop invariant of the factorial program could be "the grass is green and the sky is blue". That doesn't change no matter what we do in the factorial loop nor how many times we do it. But of course, that's useless and not the point. Obviously that's not a good choice of invariant.

The real benefit in loop invariants comes when we choose a useful one. Choose an invariant that helps us know whether we've built the loop correctly. It can even help us know whether it is executing correctly at run time. So, what we want to do is create a loop invariant Q such that

- The invariant test Q is done just before every loop exit test P,
- at every iteration of the loop, the invariant is always true for the then-current values in the loop, *and*
- that the invariant Q is the partial result of the calculation or loop body so far.

Note that this is not an `If-Then-Else` test. If it were, that would make a second exit from our loop and we don't want that. Rather, the invariant is something we consider during development and verification. With `Assert` statements, it can also be used during debugging. It would then be removed and changed to a comment in production programs. Using an `Assert` statement to check invariants is an good practice (see "The Assert method", p.126).

Loop invariant example

In our factorial example, then, the loop invariant Q will be that the current result so far, R, will equal the factorial so far of that I-th iteration: "R = I!".

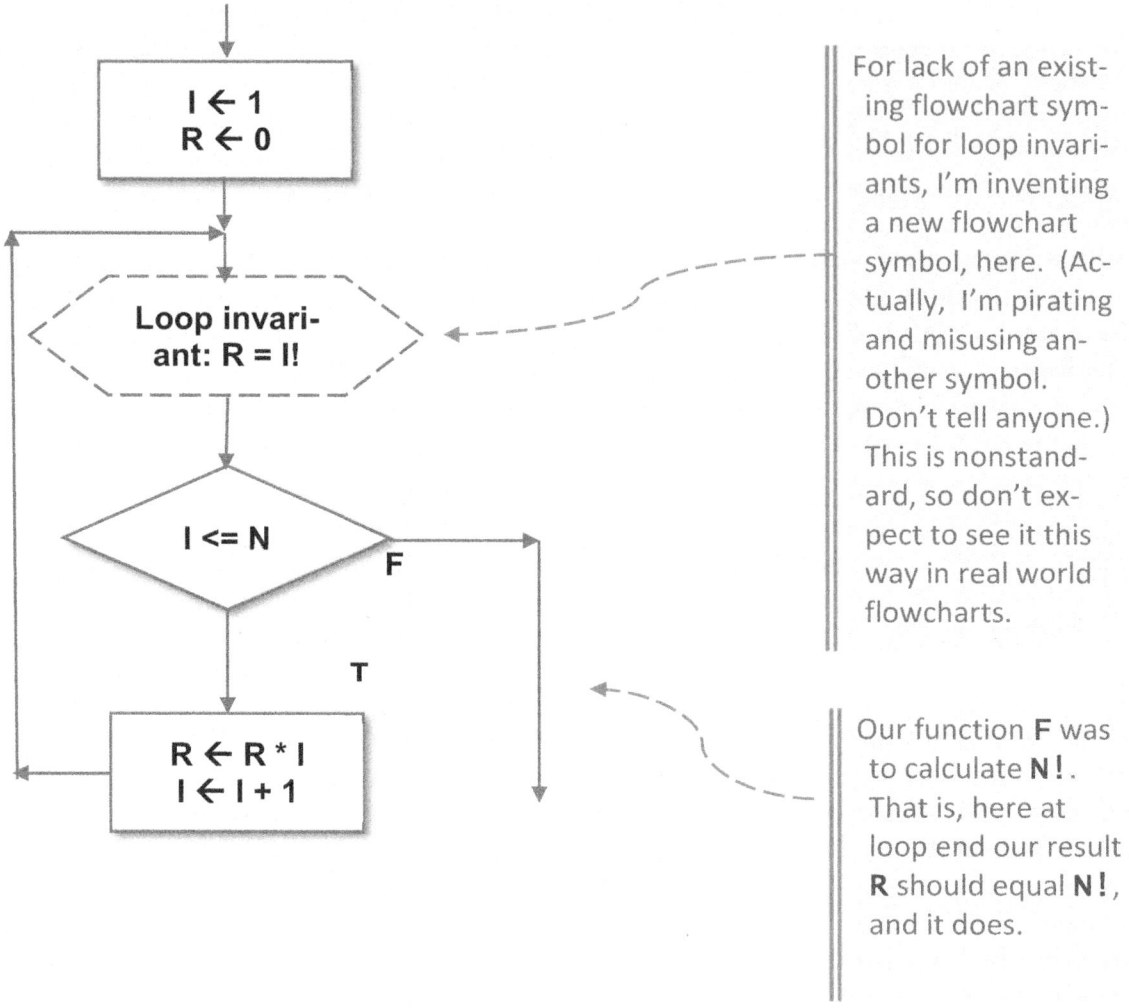

Use of loop invariants in verification

Then we can add to our verification questions:

- Is the loop invariant right? Is it the case that at every iteration, the loop invariant Q is always true?
- Does the loop invariant Q and the negation of the loop test P (i.e., and ¬P) cause loop exit with the correct answer R which is the function to be performed F?

If so, then the loop is looking good and is likely correct. (That assumes the other verification questions are answered appropriately also, of course.)

Another loop invariant example

Consider our ACL processing example. Better yet, consider the simplified Do-While example that uses essentially the same loop:

Appendix 4 – Loop Invariants

```
LN ← 0
Read Data Line from File
While not EOF Do
    {Loop invariant: Have processed all through line LN} Note-48
    LN ← LN + 1
    Process data
    Read Data Line from File
End While
```

Is it always true at the point of the loop invariant assertion that we've processed everything through line **LN**? Yes.

Is it the case that if we hit `End-of-File` and we've processed everything so far, then we've in fact processed the whole file? Yes.

So, we're good.

For the ACL example *specifically*, we might ask:

Is it always true at the point of the loop invariant assertion that we've searched the ACL file up to there? Yes.

Is it the case that if we hit `End-of-File` and we've processed everything in the ACL file so far, then we've in fact processed the whole ACL file? Yes.

And we can further ask: If we've processed the whole ACL file, then have we either

- found the ACL to show that the `User_ID` is to have valid access to the desired `Data_File`, or
- have not found either the `User_ID` or the `Data_File` listed in the ACL (in which case, the user is to be denied access)?

Yes!

So, it's good. It appears that our program is correct.

---

[48] Advanced note, feel free to skip. Some programming languages have an **ASSERT** statement for checking several things including invariants. If the invariant listed in the statement is true, fine; if not, it gives an error message and/or stops the program. Personally, I don't find such **ASSERT** statements always very useful for this. They are very useful in other contexts, however. They can be a sort of vicious circle, here. In our factorial program, for example, to evaluate the statement, `ASSERT R = I!` we'd have to evaluate `I!`. But factorial is our program, so we can't (yet) calculate it. More on **ASSERT**s in "The Assert method" of debugging, p.123.

On Programming

Appendix 5 – A word on program maintenance and debugging

> *"That tendency to err that programmers have been noticed to share with other human beings has often been treated as if it were an awkwardness attendant upon programming's adolescence, which like acne would disappear with the craft's coming of age. It has proved otherwise."*
>
> — Mark Halpern, "Computer Programming: Debugging Epoch Opens", <u>Computers and Automation</u>, Nov, 1965
>
> *"Testing shows the presence, not the absence, of bugs."*
>
> -- Edsger W. Dijkstra, during panel discussion at NATO 1969 Conference on Software Engineering Techniques
>
> *"Always code as if the guy who ends up maintaining your code will be a violent psychopath who knows where you live"*
>
> — John Woods

The time, effort, and cost for maintenance of an operational production program is much, much greater than that of developing it in the first place. This is true regardless of the size or magnitude of the program or system. That is primarily because a program or system is in use for much, much longer than it takes to develop it. (If it were otherwise, it wouldn't be worth the effort to develop it in the first place!)

That implies that maintenance and debugging are vitally important, and that when developing a program or system, it should be developed with maintenance and debugging in mind. In other words, design it from the outset to be easy to maintain later[49].

The most common types of maintenance are:

- <u>Corrective maintenance</u> – fixing defects or bugs[50]. If we discover that id doesn't work right or doesn't do what it's supposed to do, then fixing it is corrective

---

[49] Just as an aside, <u>security</u> must also be designed-in from the beginning, not slapped on at the end. That's far beyond our scope here. Nevertheless, it's amazing how many systems try to add it on later. That ultimately ends up with a more complex but still non-secure system.

[50] Sticklers generally prefer the more professional term "*program defect*" rather than "bug". After all, programs don't "catch" bugs like people catch diseases. Rather, bugs are defects unintentionally "injected" by programmers. However, I'll generally use the more common and widely used term program <u>bug</u>.

maintenance. Corrective maintenance does not alter the program's function, requirements, or efficiency. It "merely" restores it to correctly doing what it was always intended to do. This is debugging[51].

- *Perfective maintenance* – making the program better than it was. Optimizing it, making it more efficient, faster, more user-friendly, using fewer resources, and so forth. All without appreciably changing the functional requirements of what it does. This is perfective maintenance.
- *Adaptive maintenance* – adding new features or requirements. Enhancing or extending the system's function to do more than it did before is adaptive maintenance. This involves a change or upgrade to the system's requirements.

Dave Thomas and Andrew Hunt again note in *The Pragmatic Programmer*, "Code needs to evolve; it's not a static thing".

"Problems are only opportunities in work clothes."

-- Henry J. Kaiser

Debugging[52] is the corrective maintenance process of finding and fixing system defects or "bugs". (Some would say, the *art* of finding and fixing bugs.) That definition implies the two major steps in debugging:

1) *troubleshooting* – detecting or finding the defect, and

2) *repair* – fixing the defect once found.

But wait a minute! Hasn't our whole point been that if we design and build programs in the manner we've been discussing, that they will be correct and consequently bug free? Alas! We're all human, and humans make mistakes. (Unfortunately, one of the most common mistakes is getting sloppy, lax, and taking shortcuts, even when we know better.)

Note that there are (at least) two major categories of program errors:

(1) *syntax errors*, which are mistakes or misuses of the syntax of our particular programming language. Things like typos, forgetting that a `For` loop in a particular language is called a `Do` loop, that we can't use commas in long numbers like millions, etc.

---

[51] See also Wikipedia: https://en.wikipedia.org/wiki/Debugging.

[52] Computer pioneer Grace Hopper was "the second programmer on the first computer" and the inventor of the COBOL programming language. She relates the story of a moth trapped in an electromechanical relay in one of the very first computers around 1947 (see photo, here, of it taped to computer console log). That caused an early malfunction, and resulted in the term "bug" (see Software bug - Wikipedia). There are other theories of the origin of the term (even Thomas Edison used it). But I like this one the best – and there is the evidence of the bug taped to the console log.

Appendix 5 – A word on program maintenance and debugging

(2) *logic errors*, which are mistakes in the logic or structure of the program. This is regardless of what programming language they're expressed in. In other words, they're not mere syntax errors or typos. They're designing or building the program incorrectly so that what it actually does is not what we wanted it to do.

Compilers will usually find syntax errors for us, but they cannot find logic errors. Because this book on programming is language-independent, all of our debugging methods here deal with logic and structure errors, not syntax errors.

There are many techniques of debugging, a few of which include the following. Use whatever combination of techniques are appropriate for the program you're troubleshooting.

Tracing control flow

If supported by our programming language, compiler, interpreter, or editor, we can turn on "trace mode". This will show every programming language *statement or command* in turn as it is executed. So, if the program malfunctions, we'll know exactly where it was when it stopped or ran into trouble.

Tracing data flow

Similarly (if supported), we can turn on "trace data flow". This will show the *results* (and possibly even the input variables) of every programming language statement in turn as it is executed. Alternatively, it can show the results every time a variable value is changed. So, we can tell when the program started producing wrong *values* or results. Most of the time, we'd want to trace both control flow and data flow together. That way, we know both where we are in the program *and* what the results and data values are, at the same time.

Debugging mode

Trace mode mentioned above is related to debug mode, which is available in some programming languages, systems, and editors. Often, they're both enabled together. In debugging mode, the trace (above) and `Assert` (p.126) statements are enabled. When debugging is completed and our program goes into production operation, we turn off debugging mode. This "comments out" the trace, `assert`, and other debugging statements so that they are not executed. They then cause no overhead or slowdown in the production program.

Echoing particular program locations as executed

If the compiler doesn't have trace mode, we can approximate it manually by inserting `Print`, `Display`, or `Echo` statements (whatever the language calls them) in strategic locations. These `Display` statements would essentially say, "Here I am at point Z in the program. I got this far." It's probably not feasible, or at least more trouble than it's worth, to try to do this for even a majority of the statements in the program. So, the trick is figuring out optimal locations to do this. More on this below.

Echoing particular data values

Again, if the compiler doesn't have it built in, we can approximate data tracing manually by inserting similar `Print`, `Display`, or `Echo` statements in strategic locations. These would essentially say, "At this point, the value of variable X is *blah-blah-blah*." We generally combine this with control tracing by displaying something like, "I'm at point Z and right now the value of variable X is *blah-blah-blah*."

As above, the trick is figuring out optimal locations to do this.

The Wolf Fence method

One way to figure out where to put the debugging-print statements is the so-called "wolf fence" method. Suppose we're trying to find the only wolf in Alaska. We don't know where it is, but we can hear it howl. So, we build a fence down the middle of Alaska and listen. If the howl is to our right, we build another fence down the middle of the right half where the wolf is and listen again. Keep repeating *recursively* until we've narrowed it down to an area so small that we can see the wolf. The "wolf" is the as-yet unlocated program defect, error, or bug. The fences are the `Print`/`Echo`/`Display` debugging statements.

Note for the advanced: This is essentially a binary search for the error. Binary searches are very efficient. We can make this even more efficient by starting, not in the middle of our program, but in an area we know or suspect the error to be.

The Assert method

Many programming languages have an `Assert` statement. It generally looks something like this: "`Assert` *condition* [*comment*]". When the statement is executed, it tests the *condition* that's specified. If it's true, it does nothing and continues on to the next statement in the program. If the *condition* is false, the program stops and prints/displays/echoes the *comment*. (Some languages omit the *comment*, so in that case, the program just stops.)

In many languages, `Assert`s only work in debugging mode. They aren't compiled into machine code in production, so they don't slow down or interrupt completed production systems. If your language doesn't turn them off in production mode, then change them to comments when you're done debugging and transitioning to production operations.

When our language doesn't have a built-in Assert statement, we can always write an Assert subroutine (see "Subroutine", p. 77) that does what's needed.

Using `Assert` is also an excellent way to check loop (and other) invariants (see "Appendix 4 – Loop Invariants", p.119).

Appendix 5 – A word on program maintenance and debugging

The buddy method and rubber duck method

> *"Richard continued, 'What I mean is that if you really want to understand something, the best way is to try and explain it to someone else. That forces you to sort it out in your mind. And the more slow and dim-witted your pupil, the more you have to break things down into more and more simple ideas. And that's really the essence of programming. By the time you've sorted out a complicated idea into little steps that even a stupid machine can deal with, you've learned something about it yourself."*
>
> – Douglas Adams, *Dirk Gently's Holistic Detective Agency*, 1987

Buddy programming essentially is team programming or cooperative programming. The simplest (and least team-oriented) way to do this, is to just explain your program to a colleague, item by item, statement by statement, step by step. Or to explain the malfunctioning part, anyway. It's amazing how often simply explaining it makes the lightbulb go off in our own mind and we realize what's wrong. It's sort of a "not seeing the trees for the forest" thing. A bonus is if our buddy sees things and has insights that we don't; but as often as not, that isn't even necessary.

Hence, the "rubber duck"[53] method is to explain it to an inanimate rubber duck. That's right, a real, physical rubber duckie. Get a rubber duck toy and explain your program, line by line, statement by statement, to the rubber duck (they listen well and never interrupt!). It pretty much works just as well.

A note about comments, indentation, and "pretty printing"

We've discussed *Comments* in programming throughout this book. It is important to preserve the original upper-level functional black box statements. Make them into explanatory functional comments describing what the new structure block does. This is important for debugging (and for maintenance and re-engineering, if needed).

As noted above (p.30), the most critical comments are an explanation at the beginning of every major block of program code and/or every major program structure. This should tell what that specific code does or is trying to do.

Indentation is also critical for easy understanding (see "*indentation*", p.34).

---

[53] See Dave Thomas and Andrew Hunt, *The Pragmatic Programmer* in the Bibliographical Index, pp. 130ff, below.

And more

In addition, each programming language compiler or interpreter will likely have additional debugging features built in. And each program we write will have unique characteristics and needs that require other debugging techniques that we might use. So "your performance may vary".

Debugging is a big topic and an often-difficult process, and there's much more to it; but alas, that's beyond our scope. This introduction ought to be a good start, however.

Appendix 6 – What is a computer?

> *"Computer architecture [is] the 'art of designing a machine that will be a pleasure to work with.'"*
>
> – Caxton C. Foster, <u>Computer Architecture</u>, 1970

What, exactly, *is* a computer, anyway? Most people tend to sell it short. A computer is more than we think.

A <u>computer</u> isn't just a big, fast, mathematical calculator. (Okay, it's that, too.) Rather, a computer is a general-purpose symbol manipulation machine. It can do a *lot* more than just math!

More to the point, a computer is not, as most people think, just the hardware. If it were, it would be a useless chunk of iron, a boat anchor. Something like an airplane without a flight crew. Rather, a computer is

- the hardware, plus
- the software (operating system, application software, etc.), plus
- communications, plus
- data.

Without all these components, it's useless.

Von Neumann computer architecture

The computer hardware, in turn, is

- the Central Processing Unit (<u>CPU</u>),
- internal Random Access Memory (<u>RAM</u>)[54], and
- input and output (<u>I/O</u>).

Some specialized inputs and outputs are combined, such as a hard disk drive which can be both written to (output) and subsequently read (input) by the CPU.

---

[54] Incidentally, in case you hadn't noticed, the cover / frontispiece illustration is a magnetic memory core with X, Y, and sense wire windings such as were used in second generation mainframe computers. Real memory cores are tiny and can fit on the tip of a pencil. These days, RAM is semiconductor memory chips made of essentially the same stuff that CPU chips are made of.

On Programming

A simplified view of the basic architectural structure of a computer (as originally conceived of by John von Neumann in 1945) is as follows:

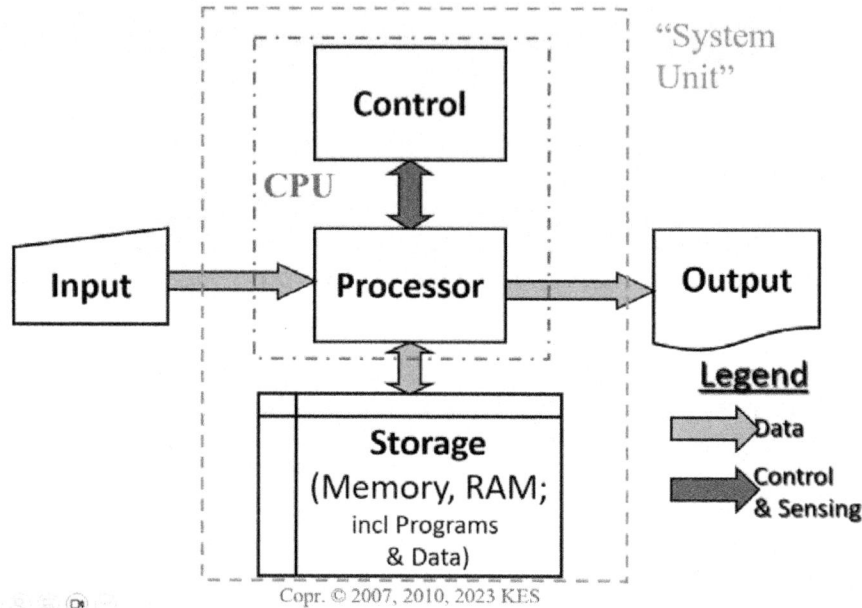

Figure 8 – Block diagram of classic von Neumann computer architecture
(by author)

A modern computer is composed of

- what is sometimes called a "system unit" and
- I/O.

I/O in turn includes

- input,
- output, and
- their I/O control units.

The system unit is composed of

- the CPU,
- main RAM storage for programs and data while being executed,
- hard disk (or Solid-State Drive, SSD) for long-term "permanent" storage,
- and cache.

The CPU is composed of

- the processor (including the arithmetic and logic unit or ALU), and
- the control unit.

Appendix 6 – What is a computer?

- It almost always also includes Read-Only Memory (*ROM*; not shown on this diagram) which is for storing *firmware* (see Wikipedia). Firmware is low-level, built-in microprogramming that runs the hardware.

Gall's Law
"A complex system that works is invariably found to have evolved from a simple system that worked…"

– *John Gall*

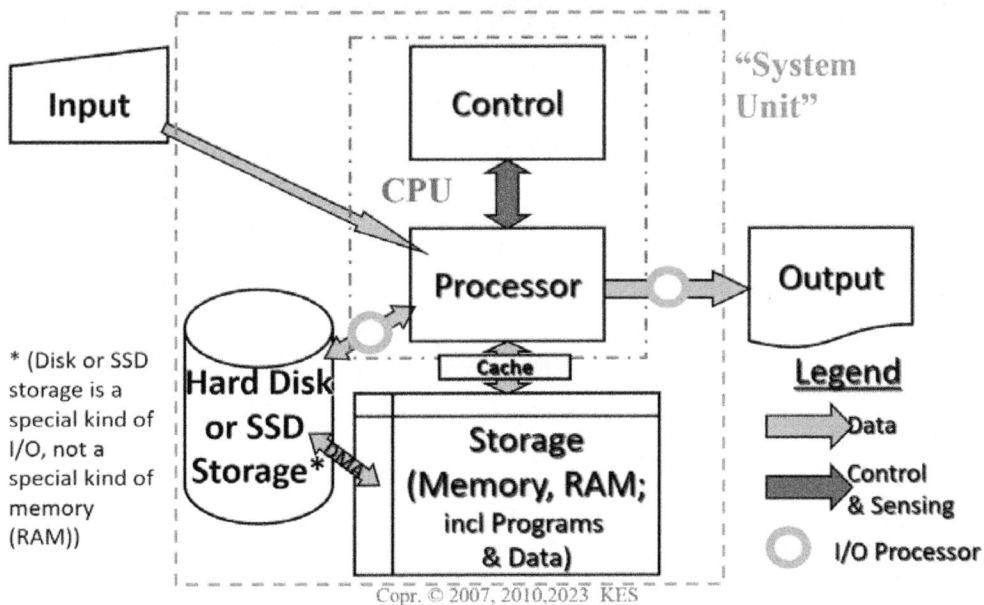

Figure 9 – Block diagram of a modern computer
(by author)

It's even more complex than this, of course. There are usually several levels of cache or fast-access scratchpad memory. The peripherals (hard disk, SSD, I/O, etc.) each have their own controller which is a small, specialized CPU of its own. The hard disk or SSD usually has "direct" access ("*DMA*") to the RAM storage via another specialized controller. There are also network interface cards or chips (which are small specialized CPUs). There are special graphics processors (graphics- and math-oriented CPUs that connect directly to the main CPU and often also to RAM); and so forth.

On Programming

Appendix 6 – What is a computer?

Computers and Information Systems hierarchy

Similarly, an *information system* *(IS)* is

- a computer, plus
- its data and communications (okay, that's a little redundant since I already mentioned those), plus
- people to operate and use it, plus
- the procedures telling how it is to be used for a particular purpose (instructions, manual, admin procedures, etc.).

A home laptop is a computer but not an information system. A bank's account management system, an employer's HR system, a supermarket's checkout and inventory management system are all examples of information systems.

Here's how it all fits together:

On Programming

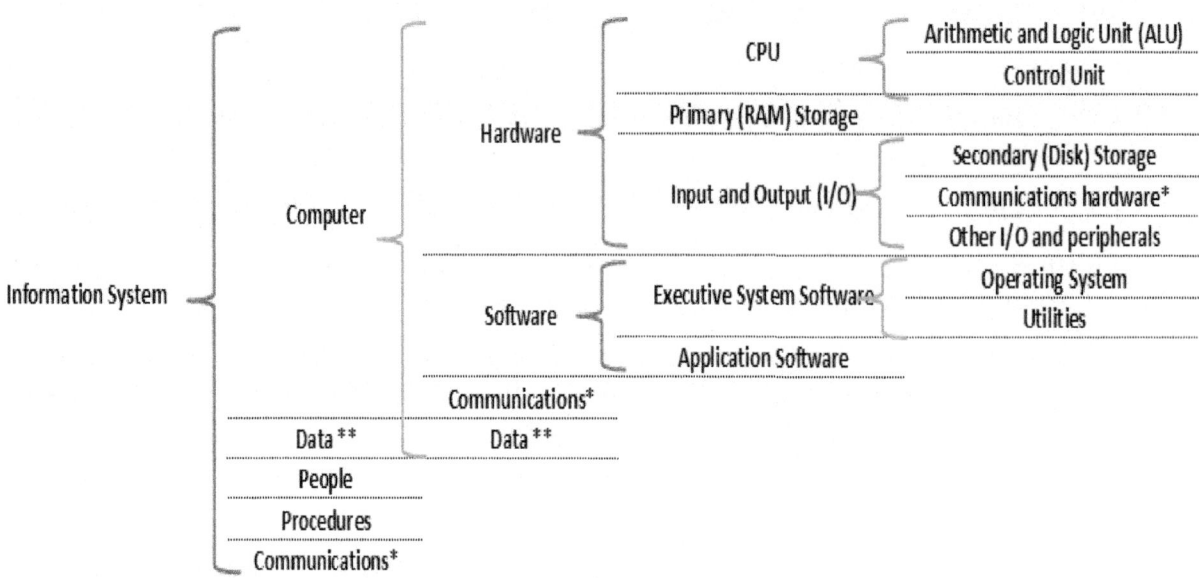

Figure 10 – Warnier-Orr diagram of IS and computer components
(by author)

(For those who like such things, we could also draw a Venn diagram of this. But that is left to the reader as an exercise.)

Appendix 6 – What is a computer?

Computer Layers and Levels of Abstraction

> *"Hardware and software are logically equivalent. ...*
> *One man's hardware is another man's software. ...*
> *There are no hard and fast rules about what must be in hardware and*
> *what must be in software."*
>
> *– Andrew S. Tannenbaum, Structured Computer Organization, 1976*

Another view, also valid, of the computer hierarchy (this time from the bottom up) is that a computer, of course, is ultimately built of ...

- *electronic circuits* of transistors working with voltages and currents, which are built into ...

- levels of *digital logic circuits* (first **And**, **Or**, and **Not** gates; then flip-flops, registers, busses, etc.), working with bits (zeroes and ones) which build ...

- levels of *microprocessors* of *firmware* and Reduced Instruction Set (RISC) processors, that implement ...

- Complex (CISC) Instruction Set Processors (ISPs[55]). This is the binary instruction codes level we usually think of as a computer, but it is a useless and inoperable chunk of iron without ...

- Operating Systems (OS) like Windows, MacOS, IOS, and Linux. (Each of these are themselves are built of layers from low level supervisory kernels to drivers and OS utilities.) The OS actually runs the computer. (As noted, without the OS, the computer is just a useless hunk of iron). Then ...

- *middleware* and other *system software* and utilities between the OS and the applications. (This includes software such as database management systems (DBMSs), compilers, graphical user interfaces (GUIs), etc.)). And finally ...

- layers of *application software* ranging from built-in or added-on apps to at last ...

- the application programs that we, ourselves, might write.

Here is a diagram showing the same thing, but from the top down:

---

[55] "ISP" can also mean Internet Service Provider, the company and systems that connect your computer to the Internet and World Wide Web. Here, we mean Instruction Set Processor. We have to distinguish the meaning by the context.

On Programming

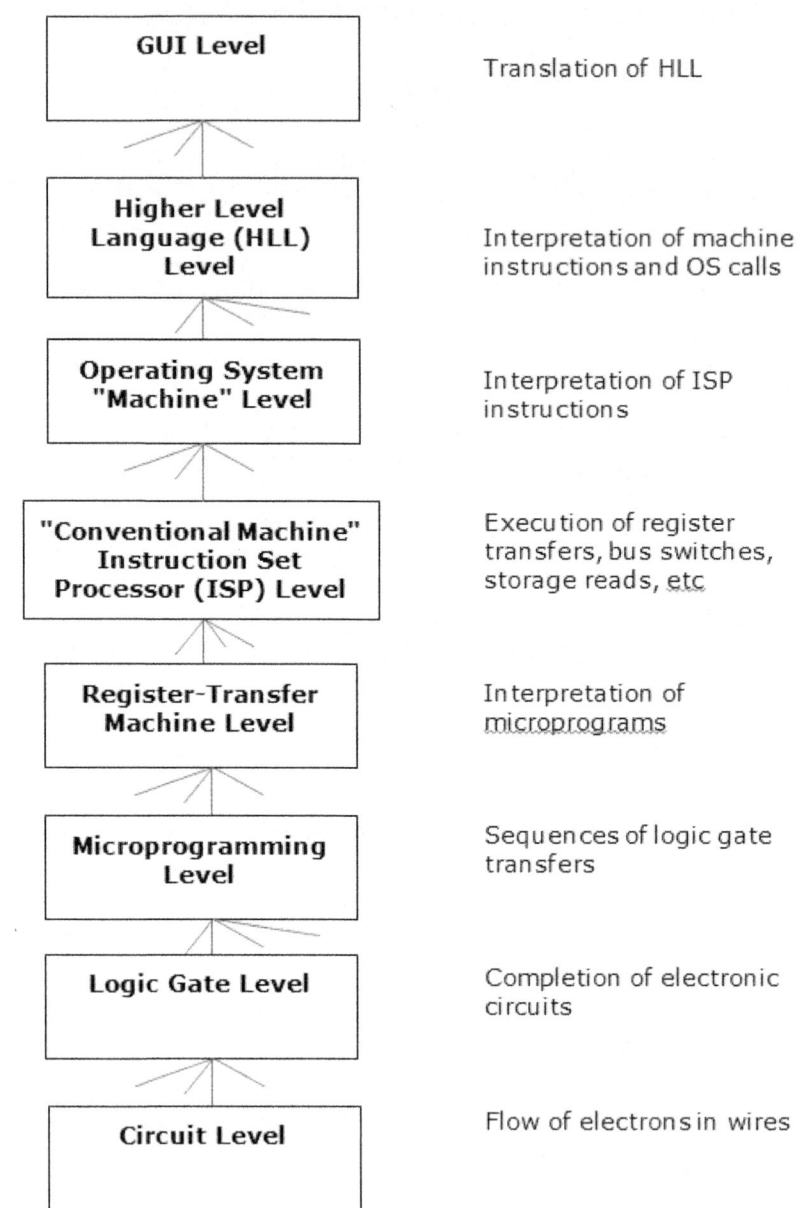

Figure 11 – *Hierarchy of Levels of Abstraction*
(by author; adapted in part from Tannenbaun 1976, Bell 1971, and Siewiorek 1982)

We can validly say that each of these levels defines both what a computer *is* and what languages and methods it is programmed in. But the truth is that a computer is *all* these levels combined and would be useless if any of them were missing.

All this, incidentally, is what gets us from the zeros-and-ones binary of the hardware (which we very fortunately *don't* have to program in), to the higher-level languages that we do program in and that are what we've been discussing in this book.

Appendix 7 – A brief introduction to systems analysis

> *"It must be remembered that there is nothing more difficult to plan, more doubtful of success, nor more dangerous to manage than the creation of a new order of things*[56]*. For the initiator has the enmity of all who would profit by the preservation of the old institution and merely lukewarm defenders in those who would gain by the new ones."*
>
> – Niccolo Machiavelli, <u>The Prince</u>, 1513

Computer <u>*systems analysis*</u> uses essentially the same top-down divide-and-conquer approach as does programming. Systems analysis, however, is applied to the design of entire information systems (see "Computers and Information Systems hierarchy", p.133). Programming is at a lower level, whereas systems and systems analysis are at a higher level. Systems analysis, of course, uses different structures, diagrams, and techniques than does programming.

There are at least two kinds of systems analysis:

- higher-level, more business- and functionally-oriented systems analysis; and
- lower-level, more technical, more design-oriented systems analysis.

The latter, lower-level process concerns primarily how to break down whole systems into lower level modules, which themselves will form or be broken down into programs. That is more oriented toward the other, non-programming, phases of the systems lifecycle.

The former, higher-level more functionally-oriented systems analysis is very general. *As well as* its forte in higher-level analysis of business functions, it is *also* useful in the initial stage of program planning ("Step 0 – Think first! Plan ahead!", p. 12). Therefore, and because of its wide, general applicability to life, a brief summary is included here.

In fact, the actual *process* of systems analysis as presented below is essentially the same as

- the processes of detective investigations,
- engineering troubleshooting,
- diagnostic medicine,
- management case studies,

---

[56] Some translations from Italian use "a new system" for "a new order of things". Perhaps that translator was a systems analyst?

- the scientific method, and more

Each of these, of course, is applied to its own domain and "database" and has its own specialized additions and uniquenesses.

The Formal Systems Approach

The classic Formal Systems Approach[57] to systems analysis is elegant in its simplicity and power. (However, it is not always quick to carry out.) As presented by Dr Lewis Branscomb former VP & Chief Scientist of IBM and former Director of NBS (NIST), it is:

> 1. What is the *apparent* problem/issue as stated?
> 2. What, after investigation, are the *facts* (and assumptions and constraints)?
> 3. What is the *real* problem[58]?
> 4. What are the alternatives (alternative solutions, alternative explanations)?
> 5. After analysis of alternatives, what is the *best* alternative or solution (or explanation)?
> 6. What course of action should be followed? (plan, recommendation)

---

[57] Branscomb's presentation of the formal systems approach, here, is also entirely consistent with George Polya's *How to Solve It: A New Aspect of Mathematical Method* (1945) – see Bibliographical Index, below, and Wikipedia article: https://en.wikipedia.org/wiki/How_to_Solve_It/

[58] It is <u>un</u>common that the *real* problem turns out to be the same as the *stated* problem!

Bibliographical Index

A brief, informal, annotated bibliography and partial index of terms and works

Abelson, Harold, et al. 1996. *Structure and Interpretation of Computer Programs – 2nd Edition*. The MIT Press. 657 pp. ISBN: 978-0262510875. A more advanced textbook that was used for introductory computer science classes at MIT, using the Lisp programming language. MIT notwithstanding, I'm not sure this text is entirely suitable for beginning students. (There are also a JavaScript version, see Henz, Martin, below; and an interactive Lisp-base version, see Xuanji, below. If you're going to use a Lisp-based version, I recommend the interactive version.)

Access Control List (ACL) – A computer file or database listing users and their authorization level for access to files. See Wikipedia: https://en.wikipedia.org/wiki/Access-control_list.

Alexander, Christopher, 1964. *Notes on the Synthesis of Form*. Harvard University Press. 224 pgs. ISBN: 978-0674627512. Primarily about building architecture and design, its concepts apply to computer and software design, too.

Basic programming language – A simplified ("basic") programming language for beginners (the "B" stands for "Beginners'"). Computer scientists tend to deprecate basic because wasn't a very good language from a computer science point of view. But, as they all tend to do, the Basic language has evolved and "this isn't your father's Basic any more". The Visual Basic versions, for instance, are now modern, object-oriented, block-structured languages that can hold their own in many arenas. See Wikipedia: https://en.wikipedia.org/wiki/BASIC.

Bentley, Jon. 1999. *Programming Pearls 2nd Edition*. Addison-Wesley Professional (2nd edition, September 27, 1999) . ISBN: 978-0201657883. A little more advanced, but a very good book, primarily about algorithms.

Brooks, Frederick – Fred Brooks is a professor of computer science and was the project manager for development of IBM's 360 computer and for its OS/360 operating system. Among many other things, he wrote *The Mythical Man-Month* and "No silver bullet: Essence and accident in software engineering." See Wikipedia: https://en.wikipedia.org/wiki/Fred_Brooks

____ Brooks 1995. *Mythical Man-Month, The: Essays on Software Engineering, Anniversary Edition Anniversary Edition* Addison-Wesley Professional (Anniversary edition (August 2, 1995). ISBN: 978-0201835953. This is an excellent book, though it does not concentrate on programming but goes far beyond. I highly recommend it.

____ Brooks 1986. "No Silver Bullet—Essence and Accident in Software Engineering". Proceedings of the IFIP Tenth World Computing Conference: 1069–1076. Also available as "No Silver Bullet—Essence and Accident in Software Engineering". IEEE Computer. 20 (4), April 1987: 10–19. An excellent article, the (oversimplified) gist of which is that we've already picked all the "low hanging fruit", so software engineering is going to be hard from here on in.

Bug – see Software Bug, below. A software defect or error. Programs don't "catch" bugs like people catch diseases; rather, bugs are defects (unintentionally) "injected" by programmers.

Capability Maturity Model (CMM) – A model to rate an organization's level of excellence in software engineering (SE) management processes. Initiated by Watts Humphrey (see below) at Carnegie Mellon University's Software Engineering Institute. Sometimes incorrectly thought to be a model for doing software engineering, it is rather for processes in SE management. See Wikipedia: https://en.wikipedia.org/wiki/Capability_Maturity_Model

Code Complete – see McConnell, Steve, below. An excellent and comprehensive book about programming, primarily for practitioners as opposed to new students. Does not replace structured programming, but to be used *with* it. Includes object-oriented programming. Examples are in several programming languages.

"Danger, Will Robinson!" – A catch phrase warning from the Robot to 9-year-old Will Robinson in the campy 1960s TV series *Lost in Space.* See Wikipedia: https://en.wikipedia.org/wiki/Lost_in_Space#Catchphrases.

Debugging – corrective maintenance to fix errors. See also https://en.wikipedia.org/wiki/Debugging.

Dijkstra, Edsger W. – A consummate early computer scientist and software engineer. See Wikipedia: https://en.wikipedia.org/wiki/Edsger_W._Dijkstra.

____ Dijkstra 1975. "How do we tell truths that might hurt?", EWD498, 18 June 1975. A list of observations about programming and especially programming languages, not all favorable.

____ Dijkstra 1969. "Structured programming", EWD268, August 1969. An early, quite possibly the earliest, paper introducing structured programming.

EDVAC ("Electronic Discrete Variable Automatic Computer") – The first stored program electronic digital computer (in 1945). Based on the *von Neumann computer architecture*. See Wikipedia: https://en.wikipedia.org/wiki/EDVAC.

Elements of Programming Style – see Kernighan, Brian, below. Though rather dated (using Fortran and PL/1), a very good book that takes real programs as examples and rewrites them to be clearer, better, and more correct.

ENIAC ("Electronic Numerical Integrator and Computer" or "... and Calculator") – The first electronic digital computer (in 1945). Programmed via plugboards and connecting cables rather than via stored programs as in the von Neumann architecture and in all modern computers. See Wikipedia: https://en.wikipedia.org/wiki/ENIAC.

Factorial – The mathematical function $N!$ that repeatedly multiplies $1 \times 2 \times 3 \times 4 \times ...$ up to N. See Wikipedia: https://en.wikipedia.org/wiki/Factorial.

Bibliographical Index

Felleisen, Matthias, et al. 2018. *How to Design Programs, second edition: An Introduction to Programming and Computing*. (HTDP). The MIT Press. 792 pgs. ISBN: 978-0262534802. An excellent and comprehensive advanced introduction to how to design computer programs oriented toward computer science. It uses a Lisp-like prefix-notation "functional programming" language, which can be powerful but daunting at first. See https://htdp.org/

Flowchart – A diagramming technique that shows actions and their connections. There are several types of flowcharts, the most common of which is a procedural flowchart, showing the flow of control between the procedural blocks in a computer program. See Wikipedia: https://en.wikipedia.org/wiki/Flowchart.

Finite State Machine (FSM) – A particular way of organizing a program or hardware that operates by transitioning from one state to another, performing functions along the way. See Wikipedia: https://en.wikipedia.org/wiki/Finite-state_machine.

Fundamental Structure Theorem – A proven principle of programming that relates flowcharts to the logic structures used to represent and implement them. Specifically: programs (any that can be flowcharted), can be programmed using only three basic control structures: Sequence, If-Then-Else, and Do-While. see Linger, Richard, et al. 1979. *Structured programming – theory and practice*.

Gauss, Edward, 1982. "The 'Wolf Fence' algorithm for debugging", *Communications of the ACM*. 25,11, 01 November 1982. https://dl.acm.org/doi/10.1145/358690.358695. A method for troubleshooting computer program errors by repetitively narrowing down their possible location.

Glass, Robert. *Software Creativity 2.0*. developer.* Books. 484 pgs. ISBN: 978-0977213313. Programming and software development from a problem-solving point of view. Highly recommended, though probably not for beginners.

Henz, Martin, MIT Electrical Engineering and Computer Science. *Structure and Interpretation of Computer Programs: JavaScript Edition*. The MIT Press. 640 pgs. ISBN: 978-0262543231. https://sourceacademy.org/sicpjs/index. The JavaScript version of SICP. (There are also a Lisp-based version, see Abelson, Harold, above; and an interactive Lisp-base version, see Xuanji, below. If you're going to use a Lisp-based version, I recommend the interactive version.)

Hopper, Grace – Rear Admiral Grace Murray Hopper, PhD, is a fascinating computer pioneer. "The second programmer on the first computer". Among other things, she was the inventor of the COBOL programming language. See Wikipedia: https://en.wikipedia.org/wiki/Grace_Hopper.

How to Design Programs (HTDP) – See Felleisen, above. An excellent and comprehensive advanced introduction to how to design computer programs oriented toward computer science. It uses a Lisp-like prefix-notation "functional programming" language, which can be powerful but daunting at first. See https://htdp.org/

How to Solve It: A New Aspect of Mathematical Method, by George Polya (1945) – A good, brief summary of the method, which is entirely consistent with Branscomb's

"The Formal Systems Approach" (p. 138). See Wikipedia article https://en.wikipedia.org/wiki/How_to_Solve_It,

HTDP – see Felleisen, *How to Design Programs*, above.

Humphrey, Watts – Former vice president and manager of software development at IBM, and professor at Carnegie-Mellon University's Software Engineering Institute (SEI), where he initiated the software engineering management Capability Maturity Model (CMM; see above). Author of Intro to the *Personal Software Process*, the *Team Software Process*, and several other books on software engineering and software development. I recommend just about anything he's written. See Wikipedia: https://en.wikipedia.org/wiki/Watts_Humphrey.

____ Humphrey 1996. *Introduction to the Personal Software Process 1st Edition*. Addison-Wesley Professional (1st edition (January 1, 1996): 278 pp. ISBN: 978-0201548099. Essentially an earlier edition of *PSP: A Self-Improvement Process for Software Engineers*. Details a process for both developing software and especially estimating how long it will take to do so. A very valuable resource for professional programmers, most of whom are typically poor estimators.

____ Humphrey 2005. *PSP: A Self-improvement Process For Software Engineers 1st Edition*. Addison-Wesley Professional (1st edition (March 15, 2005): 345 pp. ISBN: 978-0321305497. Essentially a newer edition of *Introduction to the Personal Software Process*, oriented toward professional software engineers. Details a process for both developing software and especially estimating how long it will take to do so. A very valuable resource for professional programmers, most of whom are typically poor estimators.

Isaiah 28:10-13 – A prophet's ancient observation that sounds much like modern computer programs. See Bible Gateway. http://www.biblegateway.com/passage/?search=Isaiah28:10-13&version=KJV.

Kernighan, Brian, and Rob Pike. 1999. *The Practice of Programming*. Addison-Wesley. 288 pgs. ISBN: 978-0201615869. Another good book somewhat similar in scope, though shorter in volume, to *Code Complete*. Uses several languages.

Kernighan, Brian and P.J. Plauger. 1978. *The Elements of Programming Style, 2nd Edition 2nd Edition*. McGraw-Hill. ISBN: 978-0070342071. Though rather dated (using Fortran and PL/1), a very good book that takes real programs as examples and rewrites them to be clearer, better, and more correct.

Ledgard, Henry, 1975. *Programming Proverbs: Principles of Good Programming with Numerous Examples to Improve Programming Style and Proficiency*. Hayden Book Company. ISBN: 978-0810455221. As its subtitle says, it is principles of good programming practice. It does not replace structured programming, but to be used *with* it. A little dated (uses Algol and PL/1) but good practices, nevertheless.

Linger, Richard, Harlan Mills, and Bernard Witt. 1979. *Structured programming – theory and practice*. Addison-Wesley. ISBN 978-0-201-14461-1. An excellent book concentrating on the computer science basis of structured programming, though rather pricey. For a more accessible summary, see Mills, Harlan, "How to write correct programs and know it", below.

Bibliographical Index

Lisp programming language – An unusual, non-traditional programming language used for linked list processing ("Lisp" comes from "List Processor"), for early artificial intelligence programming, teaching computer science, and the like. Lisp is based on *Polish notation* (see below). Both Lisp and prefix notation are powerful but can be daunting until we're used to them. See Wikipedia: https://en.wikipedia.org/wiki/Lisp_(programming_language).

Loop Invariant – A condition that remains (invariant) every time the test in a loop is executed. See Wikipedia: https://en.wikipedia.org/wiki/Loop_invariant.

McConnell, Steve. 2004. *Code Complete: A Practical Handbook of Software Construction, 2nd Edition*. Microsoft Press (2nd edition (July 7, 2004) . ISBN: 978-0735619678. An excellent and comprehensive book about programming, primarily for practitioners as opposed to new students. Does not replace structured programming, but to be used *with* it. Includes object-oriented programming. Examples are in several programming languages.

Mills, Harlan – A computer scientist critical to the early development of software engineering and structured programming. I recommend just about anything he's written. See Wikipedia: https://en.wikipedia.org/wiki/Harlan_Mills.

____ Mills 1975. "How to write correct programs and know it". *Proc. 1975 International Conference on Reliable Software*, Los Angeles, Apr. 21-23, 1975. IEEE Cat. No. 5CH0940-7CSR. ACM Digital Library: https://dl.acm.org/doi/10.1145/800027.808459. Also available at: https://ia801709.us.archive.org/23/items/how-to-write-correct-programs-and-know-it/How%20to%20Write%20Correct%20Programs%20and%20Know%20It.pdf. A more accessible summary of, and predecessor to, Linger, Mills, and Witt's *Structured Programming*.

Nassi-Schneiderman Chart – A type of block diagram that in some ways is simpler than a flowchart and allows only valid structures of the Fundamental Structure Theorem. See Wikipedia: https://en.wikipedia.org/wiki/Nassi%E2%80%93Shneiderman_diagram.

"No Silver Bullet " see Brooks, Frederick, "No Silver Bullet – Essence and Accident in Software Engineering". An excellent article, the (oversimplified) gist of which is that we've already picked all the "low hanging fruit", so software engineering is going to be hard from here on in.

Polish notation – A mathematical notation in which the operator comes first, rather than between the operands. See Wikipedia: https://en.wikipedia.org/wiki/Polish_notation. See also Prefix Notation, below.

Personal Software Process, and *PSP* – See Humphrey, Watts, above. Details a process for developing software and estimating how long it will take to do so. A very valuable resource for professional programmers, most of whom are typically poor estimators.

Pragmatic Programmer – An excellent and comprehensive book about programming, primarily for practitioners as opposed to new students. Does not replace structured programming, but to be used *with* it. Highly recommended. For information, see

Wikipedia: https://en.wikipedia.org/wiki/The_Pragmatic_Programmer. For the book citation, see Thomas, David, below.

Prefix notation – Polish notation or prefix notation puts the operation *before* the arguments. For example, 2 times 3 would be written (* 2 3) rather than the more familiar 2 × 3 or 2 * 3, and 4 plus 5 plus 6 would be written (+ 4 5 6) rather than 4 + 5 + 6. This is powerful but can be daunting until we're used to it. See Wikipedia: https://en.wikipedia.org/wiki/Polish_notation.

Programming Pearls – see Bentley, John, above. A little more advanced, but a very good book, primarily about algorithms.

Programming Proverbs – see Ledgard, Henry, above. As its subtitle says, its principles of good programming practice. It does not replace structured programming, but to be used *with* it. A little dated (uses Algol and PL/1) but good practices, nevertheless.

Recursion – As noted above, recursion is another form of repetition than loops. In recursion, a program (usually a subroutine) or invokes itself. See Wikipedia: https://en.wikipedia.org/wiki/Recursion, particularly see https://en.wikipedia.org/wiki/Recursion#In_computer_science.

SICP – see *Structure and Interpretation of Computer Programs*, below. There are at least three versions to choose from.

Software bug – A software defect or error. The term comes from an incident in which a moth was trapped in an electromechanical relay in one of the very first electromagnetic digital computers around 1947, caused a malfunction, and resulted in the term "bug". See photo of the console log here: https://en.wikipedia.org/wiki/Grace_Hopper#/media/File:First_Computer_Bug,_1945.jpg. Programs don't "catch" bugs like people catch diseases; rather, bugs are defects (unintentionally) "injected" by programmers. See Wikipedia: https://en.wikipedia.org/wiki/Software_bug#History.

Software engineering (*SE*) – Applying engineering approaches and techniques to the development of software. Includes development processes, usually the entire development lifecycle from systems analysis through design, construction and programming, testing, installation / implementation, and maintenance.

Structure and Interpretation of Computer Programs (SICP) – There are several versions, including the three cited herein. See:
- Abelson, Harold for the Lisp-based version;
- Henz, Martin for JavaScript-based version; and
- Xuanji, for the online, interactive Lisp-based version.

For those interested in a more advanced textbook that was used for introductory computer science classes at MIT. If you're going to use the Lisp-based version, I recommend the Xuanji online, interactive version.

Structured programming – theory and practice – see Linger, Richard, above. An early explanation of structured programming and the Fundamental Structure Theorem.

Thomas, David and Andrew Hunt, 2019. *The Pragmatic Programmer: Your journey to mastery, 20th Anniversary Edition, 2nd Edition* Addison-Wesley Professional (2nd edition (July 30, 2019) 522 pp. An excellent and comprehensive book about

Bibliographical Index

programming, primarily for practitioners as opposed to new students. Does not replace structured programming, but to be used *with* it. I recommend pretty much anything they've written.

Yourdon, Edward. 1988. *Modern Structured Analysis First Edition*. Prentice Hall. 688 pgs. ISBN: 978-0135986240. An introduction to "structured" computer systems analysis and design, for those who are interested. In spite of the title, it's no longer very "modern".

Von Neumann computer architecture – The foundational "stored program" architecture of modern computers, considerably extended and expanded since its inception by John von Neumann in the EDVAC computer in 1945. See Wikipedia: https://en.wikipedia.org/wiki/Von_Neumann_architecture.

Wolf Fence debugging method – see Gauss, Edward, "The 'Wolf Fence' algorithm for debugging", above. A method for troubleshooting computer program errors by repetitively narrowing down their possible location. See also https://en.wikipedia.org/wiki/Debugging#Techniques *"Wolf fence" algorithm*.

Xuanji. *Structure and Interpretation of Computer Programs: Interactive Version*. (undated, work in progress). For those interested in a more advanced textbook that was used for introductory computer science classes at MIT. If you're going to use the Lisp-based version, I recommend this online, interactive version. See https://xuanji.appspot.com/isicp/.

On Programming

Index to Definitions

Rather than a full glossary of definitions, this index to definitions from the text may prove of some use:

Access Control List (ACL), 139
Adaptive maintenance, 124
Algorithm, 11
API, 103
Application software, 135
Array, 94
Assignment, 36
Basic programming language, 139
Black box, 13
Boolean, 36
Boundary conditions, 46
Bug, 140
Class, 97
Comments, 30, 127
Compiler, 24
Computer, 129
Corrective maintenance, 123
CPU, 129
Data flow diagram, 21
Data structure axiom, 98
Databases, 98
DBMS, 98, 135
Debugging, 124
Declaration, 94
Declarations, 28
DMA, 131
EDVAC, 140
ENIAC, 140

Expression, 36
File, 98
Finite State Machine, 107
Firmware, 131, 135
Function, 13, 77
Fundamental Structure Theorem, 19
Heuristic, 11
I/O, 110, 129
Indentation, 34
Information system, 133
Integration testing, 16
Linked list, 96
Logic errors, 125
Loop invariant, 119
Nassi-Schneiderman Charts, 25
N-S Chart, 21
Object, 10, 97
Object-oriented, 7
Operating Systems, 135
Optimization, 106
Order of magnitude, 106
Perfective maintenance, 124
Program, 3
Pseudo-code, 21
Queue, 96
RAM, 129
Recursion, 75
Recursively, 126

Repair, 124
ROM, 131
Spaghetti code, 4
SQL, 98
SSD, 130
Stack, 96
Subroutine, 77
Subscript, 94
Syntax errors, 124
Systems analysis, 137

Table, 95
Tree, 97
Troubleshooting, 124
Typeless, 94
Types, 93
Unit testing, 16
Variable, 36
Von Neumann computer architecture, 140

Acknowledgments

Profound thanks to my mentors. They live on!

- Prof. Bernie Galler, you taught me so much! computer science, programming, the beginnings of software engineering, and of databases, and the love of the craft!

- Dr. Bert Herzog, professor and friend, you taught me computer graphics, operating systems, and the beginnings of networking.

- Prof. Harlan Mills, you taught me structured programming and software engineering, and their foundations.

- Dr. Ned Chapin, you taught me the practice structured programming and Chapin / Nassi-Schneiderman charting.

- Prof. Watts Humphrey, you taught me software engineering, software project estimation, and software project management.

- Larry Ruh, former colleague, friend, and "partner in 'crime'" (metaphorically speaking, of course!) where we used to work

and

- J Presper Eckert and John W Mauchley (whose son Jim, I knew), and John von Neumann, and Grace Hopper. They started it all. Without them we wouldn't have a computer industry today.

You will all be missed!

- And of course, my wife and family and God, who are always supportive, and without whom I'd be nothing.

Finally,

- My wife, who proofread this
- Jim Fowler, who helped me publish it
- David Cledanor, who encouraged me to pursue it to publication

On Programming

Author

Karl Schank is a programmer at heart. With degrees in Computer Information and Control Engineering (AKA Computer Science and -Engineering), his first career was as a computer practitioner, doing computer programming, systems analysis, management, and project management for the government.

Professor Schank's second career was teaching a broad range of computer science, information systems, IS management, and IT project management for the University of Maryland University College (now University of Maryland Global Campus), both in person and online. He had the privilege of having students on all six continents except Antarctica and was just waiting for that one!

Now retired, Karl Schank still does recreational, utility, and so-called "productivity" programming, teaches Bible study classes, and spends time with his wonderful family in Texas.

kspubs.com

On Programming

Printed in Great Britain
by Amazon